To: /

Enjoy

Allan Waddy
28/6/2019

Buckshot &
Johnnycakes

Allan W. Waddy
(a.k.a., Johnnycakes)

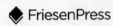 FriesenPress

Suite 300 - 990 Fort St
Victoria, BC, V8V 3K2
Canada

www.friesenpress.com

Copyright © 2018 by Allan W. Waddy
First Edition — 2018

Poem 'The Island' Written by Gloria Rose Waddy

ISBN
978-1-5255-2628-2 (Hardcover)
978-1-5255-2629-9 (Paperback)
978-1-5255-2630-5 (eBook)

1. BIOGRAPHY & AUTOBIOGRAPHY, PERSONAL MEMOIRS

Distributed to the trade by The Ingram Book Company

Dedication

To my lovely wife, Gloria Rose:
Proverbs 31:10

Chapter 1
A Life of Adventure

"So, how far is it really, Buckshot?" I murmured to my best friend.

"Not far, Johnnycakes," was his standard response to questions that, in his mind, were redundant; he was a man of few words.

Sighing in exasperation, my mind flashed back to the past.

Buckshot and Johnnycakes, now married with children of their own, had met at the age of eleven. They were always on an adventure, whether it was scouting, winter camping, looking for relics and antiques, fishing in Cowichan Bay or the inside passage of Vancouver Island, hunting for local game, or just hanging around, looking for excitement.

Buckshot and I met in September 1958 at the Quamichan Scout Hut located in the old community hall on the corner of Maple Bay and Quamichan Lake roads.

Since that very first meeting, we became inseparable and lifelong friends. It was an odd attraction, as we were total opposites, especially in personality; his father had nicknamed him "Buckshot" when he was two years old because he was everywhere in the room at once and out of sight the moment your eyes were off him. On the other hand, I was nicknamed "Johnnycakes" by his father the first time I went to Buckshot's home on Beech Road. My family nickname at that time was "Johnny," hence the name "Johnnycakes," which was derived from the bannock cakes made by the local First Nations who settled in the Cowichan Valley thousands of years before the white settlers arrived in the "Warm Land."

Buckshot lived in a beautiful old mansion on the corner of Beech and Trunk roads. The spacious property had a curved driveway that entered from Beech and exited onto Day Road.

The yard was secluded and filled with trees. I recall that Buckshot's father had erected a large canvas-wall tent on the northwest side of the property that was filled with antique cars—old cars that we played on long before we were legally able to get a driver's Licence. Buckshot's dad was into everything: logging, mining, antique second-hand stores, and everything else that could be acquired through a *deal.* In fact, Buckshot had been weaned on antiques and "special finds" long before I met him in 1958. He loved searching for arrowheads and First Nations artifacts on the shores of the inland waters, and his lifelong dream was to become an archeologist. His bedroom was filled with exotic riches, from African spears to First Nations drums, fossil rocks, and anything to do with the ocean. Buckshot spent his entire life going to garage sales and selling his treasures, which he lovingly referred to as "the junk that will make me a millionaire."

I remember the first time that I stepped into his large and spacious bedroom in the old mansion. Standing in the doorway, I became overwhelmed with the variety of objects in the room. For example, there were glass jars of marbles filled to the brim with cats' eyes, crystals, steelies, and large bull fudgers; every marble was a different color and composition. There was also a Civil War bugle with a green tassel wrapped around the handle, a metal breastplate and chainmail suit of armor, and African spears crisscrossed in front of an assegai shield. I also recall stuffed birds, a snake skin in the beak of a large brown owl, and a huge pickle jar stuffed with one, two, five, and ten–dollar bills. It took me years to appreciate all his treasures, as each artifact was more captivating than the other. He was a consummate collector of everything and anything. If you needed something, Buckshot had it somewhere in his room or yard. He was like a human crow, constantly searching for and collecting everything and anything that was shiny, of interest, or unique.

Several months after I joined the Quamichan Scout Troop, my father, Robert Waddy—a 1942 Dieppe Raid survivor and former prisoner of war—started the Second Duncan Scout Troop, located in the Saint John's Anglican Church on Jubilee Street in downtown Duncan.

After Dad opened the troop, Buckshot and I transferred there and both earned significant scouting awards.

In fact, in 1962, Buckshot became the first "Queen Scout" in the Cowichan Valley since the early 1940s—an achievement that greatly pleased my father. Not only was Buckshot my father's first Queen Scout, but he also earned his Gold All Around Cord and Bushman's Thong—a rare and coveted award in the scouting organization, thereby setting a high standard for the other boys in the district. I also earned my All Around Cords between 1961 and 1963 and received my Queen's Scout Award in 1963, which was presented to me by the lieutenant governor, Major-General George Pearkes, at Government House in Victoria. These were indeed proud moments and are still fond memories.

Some of the best memories that I have with Buckshot are scouting activities between 1958 and 1963. Not only did Buckshot and I go on camping trips with the troop, but we also spent every opportunity camping in the Valley and on Salt Spring Island. We camped everywhere there was a patch of trees near a lake or river. We would pack our grub and outdoor gear and race off on our bikes the minute school closed on Friday afternoon. Summertime was always a blur. Upon locating a rustic and secluded camp-site, we would build a lean-to from boughs and windfall poles, make a large reflector fire, and get our bedrolls laid out for the night. Buckshot loved building reflector fires, and as we were laying out the fire pit and wind break he would say, in his singsong voice, "Get her rippin', Johnnycakes"—an expression he used for the rest of his life.

Buckshot had a unique way of answering questions, and he often spoke in riddles when the mood came upon him. If I were to phone him at home and ask where he had been or what he had done that particular day, he would crypti-cally respond, "Oh, around and about, in and out, and here and there." He had a belief from a very early age that he "told no stories" and "took no prisoners" when referring to his adventures and early logging days. He was indeed a most unique and uplifting person. Our childhood and adult years were filled with endless exploits. He was a true friend and sidekick.

***

In the fall of 1960, our Scout Troop went on a ropes and lashing training camp on Maple Mountain in the Samson Narrows. The theme for the camp was designing and erecting a timber bridge made from poles lashed together. Of course, Buckshot was in charge of the operation, as he was one of the Senior Scouts at that time. I recall that on the first Saturday night, after a long and hard day of bridge construction, my father called a campfire ceremony.

In the semi-darkness, I was sitting across from Buckshot in the firelight, as we were in different patrols. Then I noticed him stealthily creep from the fire into the pitch-black evening.

Several minutes later, we heard a thundering crash from the forest and saw Buckshot racing back into the firelight with his blue jeans down around his ankles. To the utter amazement of the entire troop, Buckshot breathlessly blurted out his one and only story, which went something like this: "Man, there's something big and hairy out there; when I was bending over the latrine something licked my backside." His eyes were the size of saucers, and I recall the stunned silence around the campfire, as

Buckshot was not one to exaggerate. Black bears were common in that area.

For years, Buckshot and I rode our CCM bikes—resplendent with large black metal carriers attached to the front "V" handlebars—up and down the Island. When Buckshot was about fifteen, he got a job working in the produce department at the local Safeway store. Shortly after he started working there, I learned that he had taken the job so that he could feed his rabbits, which he kept beside the old canvas tent in the backyard. I remember that we had empty cardboard apple boxes in our bike carriers so that we could load our carriers with day-old produce. Buckshot not only got paid from his part-time job, but he also fed his rabbits on a healthy diet of Safeway greens.

Fond memories such as these brought me back to the moment of looking for the boat in the bush.

We were bumping through the forest in his one-ton pickup truck, which was filled with the fishing gear, logging equipment, power saws, ropes, pulleys, gas cans, and a myriad of odds and sods that he always carried in the bed of his company vehicle. Sitting in the front passenger seat, I became aware of the undergrowth branches as they slid along the side of the truck, and of the rocky, uneven logging road overgrown with alder trees that whipped across the windshield, slapped at the side windows, and literally tossed the truck from one side to the other. It was not hard to see that Buckshot had been a logger for most of his life and knew just about everything about falling and hauling trees, repairing second-hand equipment, and making a fast buck from his entrepreneurial exploits. Being his opposite, I was somewhat of a clothes dandy, as I had joined the Royal Canadian Navy at the age of eighteen; after working week-ends and summers in several local sawmills on Vancouver Island, the romance of the high seas lured me into military service. As similar as we were, there were subtle differences in our personalities; for example Buckshot only spoke when he had something profound to say, while I, Johnnycakes, a passionate adventurer who had crossed the Atlantic Ocean at the age of seven in a decommissioned Korean troop ship, was a constant and consummate storyteller. Regardless of our individual mannerisms, we were both born in May and shared the same values of loyalty and adventure. In fact, we were often considered the "odd guys" at a very early age.

As we bounced along towards an unknown destination, Buckshot suddenly jammed on the brakes, bringing the truck to a sudden stop, looked out his window, pulled out a tobacco pouch, and laboriously began fashioning a homemade cigarette (which was another facet of his calm and lackadaisical demeanor). Looking at him across the cab of the truck, I asked, with eager anticipation: "So, what surprises are we going to find in that thicket, Buckshot?"

He responded in his singsong and casual drawl, "A boat, so that we can go out fishing."

With mounting apprehension and a slight tremor in my voice, I pitched the next question, "So, when was the last time that you actually saw this boat?" This question had precipitated from my knowledge that Buckshot had a propensity of hiding and dumping his possessions anywhere that he happened to be at that particular moment.

His response was not surprising. He turned his head, finished twisting the rollie, stuck it in his mouth, and while lighting the cigarette, responded, "About five or six years ago, when I logged the rest of my Island."

Now, the agony really started to creep through my body as I envisioned crashing and thrashing around in the forest, looking for a fishing boat that was several miles from the ocean. In fact, various thoughts came to mind as I groaned in trepidation of finding this mysterious boat— which, in past experience, was most likely full of leaves, dirt, and maybe even holes. Not to mention, it most likely weighed hundreds of pounds and was held together by rope, patched wood, and fiberglass.

With a chuckle, Buckshot jumped out of the truck, slapped back the alder saplings, and started rummaging in the back of his pickup for a power saw. While Buckshot searched for the equipment, I painfully recalled how I had fractured my neck and lower spine in 1967 while serving in the Navy. Although full of osteoarthritis, I still managed to live an active life—as long as the physical activities were carefully controlled.

Buckshot, on the other hand, was an incredibly powerful man whose physical strength derived from over fifty years of hard physical work; in fact, I had seen him carry a sixty-pound power saw in his left hand while using his right hand to climb a huge fir tree. If the tree was dense and full of branches, he would tie a rope around the power saw, climb the tree, and then haul the saw up into the tree with his left hand. His hands were huge and covered with callouses from years of working in the logging industry. Buckshot possessed amazing strength for a five-foot-nine man. However, at times he was oblivious of my injuries and resultant physical limitations, and he quite often would demand that I "pull or push harder."

As we trudged into the forest on this particular day, Buckshot thrashed around while whipping and whacking at alder and maple saplings while I casually leaned against an old growth fir tree with the circumference of a navigational bell buoy.

"Ah-ha," bellowed Buckshot as he located the forty-year-old fifteen-foot wood and fiberglass boat in the underbrush. The smile on his face was surely an indictment that faith was more than just a word and that old boats last forever. Gingerly stepping over to the pile of debris that was supposed to be a fishing boat, I involuntarily shuddered at the thought of dragging the heavy, wet, and half-decayed monstrosity out of the woods.

"Say, Buckshot, how do you propose we get this thing out of the bush and to the ocean, which seems to be about two miles east of us?" I asked.

With a chuckle, Buckshot drawled, "We're going to drag this puppy through the forest and launch her at the lighthouse."

Having known Buckshot since our early days of fishing in the late 1950's, it was easy to see the struggle ahead. The thought of laboring the next five or six hours through the dense forest brought up old and painful memories of dragging his twelve-foot clinker-built dory into the ocean at Cowichan Bay during early morning fishing runs in July and August of 1959.

That particular memory refers to a time when Buckshot and I would roar along in his twelve-foot dory in the predawn on our way to the salmon fishing grounds at Cowichan Bay. It was only through the kindness of his mother Kay that we made it to Cowichan Bay at 4:00 a.m., as she would drive us and our gear to the Bay and then pick us up later in the afternoon.

On one of these occasions, Buckshot let me operate the motor for the very first time, so that he could sit up front and ready the fishing gear. Twelve years old and extremely nervous, I grasped the engine tiller and cranked her up to full speed, as ordered by "Sea Captain" Buckshot. Every few minutes, Buckshot would yell into the wind, "Watch where you're going, Johnnycakes."

Of course my response, which he could not hear over the wind, was, "Yeah sure, Buckshot, I'm not an idiot, you know."

Seconds later, and before the words could reach him, the boat rose out of the water at the bow, followed by a loud *thunk* as the motor flew up even with the transom then slowly went back in the water and sputtered to a stop. Buckshot shot forward out of his seat, dropped the fishing gear, and looked stunned as we drifted in the dark. "What the hell did you do, Johnnycakes?" he roared from his hands and knees.

Looking around and trying to get my bearings, I gulped and squeaked out an unintelligible response.

Before I could gather my wits, Buckshot yelled, "You ran over a huge log . . . Get up here and pick up this fishing gear."

I crawled timidly to the front of the small boat while Buckshot moved to the stern; then he pulled the motor out of the water and with an explosive grunt, wrapped his huge thirteen-year-old hands around the prop, gritted his teeth, and bent it back in place.

He had sweat popping out on his forehead, which I could now see in the light of the quickly approaching dawn. As I was trying to think of an excuse for what had happened, Buckshot pointed to a huge log drifting about three feet off the starboard side of the boat. I knew that I had been caught, so I made the decision to keep quiet. I bowed my head and pretended to sort out the tangled mess of fishing lures, while Buckshot, obviously annoyed with me, lowered the motor back in the water and yanked on the frayed starter cord.

Silently, I prayed for the welcoming noise of the twenty-year-old 9.9-horsepower *Seagull* outboard motor. Instantly, we heard a load roar and Buckshot took over the operation of the boat. For the next ten minutes, I kept my head down, still busy with the tangled mess that I had unwittingly created.

After an inordinately long silence, Buckshot said, "Johnnycakes, if you are ever going to learn about seamanship, you need to listen and pay attention." He then looked right at me and in a softer voice asked, "Do you want me to fix the gear?"

I knew then that I had been forgiven, and we gingerly switched places, allowing me a second chance at the helm.

***

Returning to the present on the logging road near the lighthouse, I realized that Buckshot was again determined to drag the boat to the ocean. We set about clearing the undergrowth from around his prize, and using a block and tackle, we heaved the behemoth out of the bush.

Alas—it soon became apparent, to my utter disappointment, that Buckshot had no intention of dragging the boat to the ocean behind his truck. So, with a simultaneous grunt, we started hand dragging the boat towards the logging road and the sea.

Hours later, exhausted but in anticipation of going sockeye fishing, we arrived at the edge of the shore overlooking the lighthouse bay. The view was spectacular; we were looking out at the Johnstone Strait and Buckshot's eighty-eight-acre island—called Turn Island—across the channel. The lighthouse was off to the right, and Buckshot made a decision to launch the boat at the government wharf, as he knew the lighthouse keeper and his wife.

Rock Bay was to the immediate north and approximately a mile and a half west of his island. The plan was to launch the boat, go back for the truck, gather up the gear and provisions, and then run over to the island—hopefully all before the evening fishing run and the change of tide.

Lowering the boat down the thirty-foot cliff was not as easy as initially anticipated; the lighthouse keeper decided to sun bathe while we struggled. Eventually, the boat landed on the beach.

With mutual sighs of contentment, we looked out to sea. Then, with a groan, I expostulated, "Buckshot, the tide is out. We need to drag the boat two hundred feet farther."

By this time, Buckshot was sitting in a lawn chair nursing a cold beer, and it was evident from the sudden and drastic change of plans (a sarcastic thought came to mind) that a sailor, logger, and lighthouse keeper could not have organized the launching better.

It was a rare occasion that Buckshot missed the mark. In fact, he was a profound thinker and planned everything in great detail. Besides logging all his life, Buckshot loved the ocean and was an experienced charter fishing guide.

He once said that he had saltwater in his veins and could happily spend his entire life on the ocean. It seemed odd that Johnnycakes had gone to sea as a career sailor, and Buckshot, who had always loved the sea, had spent his life whacking down trees. Throughout our lifelong friendship, I often ruminated how maybe there was sawdust as well as saltwater in his veins.

Exhausted and sitting in a lawn chair, I fervently hoped that the lighthouse keeper would invite us to dinner and lodge us for the night in one of the federal outbuildings. Alas, this didn't happen, and after a few minutes of restful repose, Buckshot headed back for the truck and gear.

Around 7:30 p.m., several hours before sunset, the two of us finally dragged the heavy fiberglass boat into the surf and loaded to the gunnels with provisions, fishing gear, and personal items, Buckshot repeatedly and unsuccessfully pulled the outboard starter cord.

After not hearing the comforting rumble of the outboard motor, Buckshot finally admitted that the motor probably needed a tune-up. We struggled against the surf, trying to keep the boat (and everything we had brought) off the rocks. I was near exhaustion.

About fifteen minutes later, the motor roared to life and clouds of thick blue smoke billowed into the air. In utter despair, I laid down in the boat, noticing for the first time that we had water seeping in through some cracks.

My rest was short-lived, as Buckshot said that he needed me in the bow of the boat as a lookout - as the night had suddenly turned dark and overcast. To my utter dismay, we began motoring into a summer rainstorm.

***

The unexpected squall we encountered that day reminded me of a story Cheryll, Buckshot's wife, had told me around the time they had bought the island. While moving onto the island, Buckshot had wanted a deep freezer in which he could store meat, fish and wild game. After loading and lashing the heavy deep freezer into their fifteen-foot shallow-hulled Boston Whaler, they headed off to Turn Island.

As they rolled back and forth in the surging five-foot waves and rain pelted them in the face, Buckshot yelled in the wind to his wife, "Hang onto the freezer and don't let go." Cheryll said that she was terrified that the freezer would go over the side with her hanging on for dear life. It was routinely said that to know Buckshot was to love him—but you had to forgive him for the tremendous value he placed on garage sale bargains.

***

Within minutes of launching away from the perilous rocks near the lighthouse, the sky opened up into a cloud-burst of squalling rain. The patched and vintage boat—another back-yard bargain—began rocking and rolling in the thunderstorm. Not totally aware of the danger we were in, we surged out into the channel with the storm at our backs, turned at the point, and raced the overloaded sea craft into the bay on the inside of Turn Island. The good thing was that the inside passage of Buckshot's island is approximately eight hundred yards west of East Thurlow Island and is also well sheltered from the strait.

As we approached the sheltered bay at the north end of the island, the first things visible in the semi-darkness were derelict logging trucks, derricks, cranes, diesel fuel bowsers, and thirty-year-old logging equipment. It wasn't pretty, but once the eyes could escape the remnants of the logging days of yore, the beauty of the island was—and is—breathtaking.

As the boat shot into the natural harbor and we approached a nest of half-submerged logs held together by boom chains, I gingerly leapt onto the floating dock, tied up the boat, and began unloading the gear.

Years before in 1984, Buckshot had set up an old trailer on the island, dug a well, and brought in a generator. Having been absent from the island for several years, we had no idea what to expect from the wildlife, land pirates, or local fishing boats. By the time the camp was set up and the woodstove roaring with gusto, we discovered that the generator needed repair. Not being daunted by this additional setback, it was decided that fresh fish and chips would lighten the evening's despair.

Setting out to sea again in a light rain, Buckshot navigated over to the kelp beds on the west side of the island, and soon enough, we caught a good-sized lingcod for dinner.

This was achieved by lowering a small cod jig to the ocean floor in anticipation of hooking a rock cod. After about fifteen minutes of gently rocking from side to side in the stationery boat on the ebb tide, Buckshot reeled a rock cod into the boat, which he attached to a bigger cod jig and then lowered the smaller fish to the bottom.

While we were waiting for a lingcod to take the bait, Buckshot explained, "The much larger fish will eagerly suck the smaller fish into its mouth, and when pulled to the surface, the greedy lingcod will stubbornly hang on to the smaller fish." The average lingcod in the straits are between eight and twenty pounds. Within several minutes of lowering the line, we caught a ten-pound lingcod.

After returning to the island, we quickly devoured a feast of succulent lingcod and homemade fried potatoes. After cleaning up the rustic kitchen, we played a few hands of crib in the glowing candlelight and reminisced about our many years of camping, fishing, and hunting on Vancouver Island.

With contented sighs and the anticipation of more island adventures in the morning, we tucked in for the night. The last thing I recalled before falling asleep was the haunting and forlorn hooting of an owl and the sound of deer munching twigs at the open window beside my cot.

Chapter 2
Johnnycakes: The Early Years

Vancouver Island is nestled in the Pacific Ocean on the far west coast of Canada. The inland passage of the Island is well protected. The Straits of Juan de Fuca come in from the Pacific Ocean, curving around the bottom of the Island into Active Pass and eventually merging into the Johnstone Straits. The Island is serviced by numerous ferries via Active Pass and the outlying Gulf Islands. British Columbia's capital city is Victoria, located at the bottom of Vancouver Island. The rapidly growing Island population is around 750,000. The Island is about 460 kilometers long and 100 kilometers wide at the widest point. The Island is wrapped in rugged shoreline and dotted with stunning beaches, waterfalls, and river outlets.

The interior of Vancouver Island is scattered with small rolling hills, majestic mountains, and beautiful clear lakes. The Cowichan Valley, located approximately one hour northwest of Victoria, was given its name by the local First Nations people, and its meaning is "Warm Land." It is well named, as Vancouver Island is considered to be one of the most temperate islands in the world, giving rise to west-coast rainforests that are abundant with wildlife and lush with old-growth trees, ferns, and thick undergrowth. Small island deer, magnificent Roosevelt elk, cougars, wolves, and black bears are common sightings. Smaller mammal species and abundant birdlife (including trumpeter swans) bring added joy and dimension to anyone wandering the terrain. The Island is and always will be a treasure trove of beauty and adventure, delighting the old and young alike.

The prominent lakes of the Cowichan Valley are Cowichan, Mesachie, Bear, Somenos, Quamichan, Fuller, Dugan, and Shawnigan. Cowichan Lake is on the western side of the Island and empties to the west into the Pacific Ocean through the Nitinat River and east through the Cowichan River into Cowichan Bay. The Cowichan River is approximately forty-seven kilometers long and is a source of numerous recreation and fishing activities. Cowichan Lake is a popular camping and fishing area and the lake is inhabited with cutthroat, rainbow, brown, and Dolly Varden trout.

The small village of Honeymoon Bay is located approximately three kilometers northwest of Mesachie Lake and the former mill site for Western Forest Products. The remnants of the old log dumps can be seen on the shores of Honeymoon Bay.

Gordon Bay is the home of the local area's provincial park. The tall, majestic trees within the campground and park were planted by German prisoners of war who were interned in the area during hostilities with Germany. After the war, several of the POWs remained in the area and contributed significantly to the operation of the local saw mills.

In 1953, the Honeymoon Bay Scout Troop—under the leadership of the Scout Leaders Robert Stranick and my father, Bob Waddy—organized the troop to clear and build the original nine campsites near the shore on the lake at Gordon Bay. Currently, there are more than 165 campsites open to the public year round.

Across the lake and northeast of Baldy Mountain, the small village of Youbou sits on the sunny eastern side of the lake. Youbou is the former site of the British Columbia Forest Products sawmill. Although the sawmills no longer operate on the lake, the three former mills leave an indelible mark on the landscape and communities.

Honeymoon Bay was settled in the 1880s by a pioneer farmer named Henry March who brought his English bride to the area on their honeymoon. March's farm is still standing near Gordon Bay Provincial Park. Also, the March Meadows Golf Course now sits on Sutton Creek, which was formerly a part of March's farm.

The town of Lake Cowichan is approximately seven kilometers east of Honeymoon Bay and at the foot of the lake. In the early 1950s, the locals referred to Lake Cowichan as "the foot" when going into Lake Cowichan to acquire provisions from the local merchants. Lake Cowichan is the fork in the road that accesses Youbou at the other side of the lake. The three sawmills on the lake were located at Mesachie, Honeymoon Bay, and Youbou.

Local folklore says that in 1882, John Humphreys settled in the Cowichan Valley with his crew of railroad workers and had the good fortune of meeting and marrying the Quamichan First Nations princess. In 1910, the Dominion of Canada set up a cavalry post in the City of Duncan. An historic train station now houses the local museum in Duncan's downtown core.

The combined population of the Cowichan Tribes makes it the largest First Nations band in British Columbia. Portions of the City of Duncan are constructed on land leased from the Cowichan Tribes band.

The North Cowichan Forest Museum is located several kilometers north of Duncan on the Island Highway, and it comprises an inventory of railway and logging machinery: early steam engines, donkey engines, spar trees, railway speeders, a crummy (small bus used to transport workers to logging sites) and a museum rich with photographs and personal items donated to the museum. There is a time capsule stored on the site consisting of scouting artifacts that is scheduled to be opened in the future. Somenos Lake is directly behind the museum and can be seen from the highway. A new shopping mall named the "Commons" was recently opened, and it faces towards the riparian marshes of Somenos Lake.

Maple Bay and Cowichan Bay are located directly to the east of Duncan, and they sit on the inlands waters of the straits. On the fork in the road near Quamichan Lake (Maple Bay is to the left) used to stand a large and gnarled oak tree; history tells us that the "Hanging Judge"— Matthew Begbie, who presided on the Supreme Court between 1858 and 1866— regularly carried out the death penalty using this local hanging tree. To the right of the former hanging tree is the road to Cowichan Bay, which traverses the Indian Reserve and passes directly by the Cowichan Bay Estuary, where the Cowichan River empties into the ocean.

My wife, Gloria Rose Waddy, wrote a poem about Vancouver Island as a submission to a local *Verse and Vision* literary and art display. This beautiful poem embodies much of our love for the Island:

The Island

You came to the Island for treasure,
She gave to you all you could hold
And cradled your mind in her leisure
And awakened the dreams in your soul.
You stood in her window at sunset,
Watched the swans on her gray ocean mirror
And the wings of your heart unfolded in love
And your dreams found a harbor from fear.
Come home to the Island, my dreamer,
Where the new growth of trees shines with rain
And I wait beneath soft downy covers
To lie in your arms once again.

My family has lived in the beautiful province of British Columbia for three generations since my grandfather emigrated from England to North Vancouver in 1919. My immediate family moved to Honeymoon Bay in 1949, when my father got a job working in the Western Forest Industries Sawmill operating on Cowichan Lake. We lived in a float house on the Bay, close to the log dump and beside the Sawmill. My mother,

Audrey, worked in the Mill Cookhouse and my sister and I spent the next nine years living on the lake. When my sister was born in 1946, our father had only been liberated from a German POW camp for thirteen months. My sister and I were born in North Vancouver, as was our father and his siblings.

There were stressful times in the early postwar days, as Dad was suffering undiagnosed post-traumatic stress disorder as a Second World War veteran. He was a former Olympic boxer and powerful swimmer, and he encouraged my sister and me to swim at an early age; as our parents feared that we would fall into the lake from our float house.

In an effort to teach us to swim, Dad would drop us off the edge of our boathouse into about fifteen feet of water and say, in a firm voice, "Thrash your hands and feet, keep your heads above water, and swim towards me."

I remember that our mother was horrified; she could not swim, as she had been raised near Brighton Beach, Sussex, England, where the English Channel was usually too cold for swimming.

Before we were nine years old, my sister and I could swim across the lake. The three of us would start out on the mile-and-a-half swim, my sister and I on either side of our father. Every ten or fifteen minutes, we'd take a rest while treading water.

We enjoyed many years of swimming in the lake and grew into little otters. In fact, I used to swim the Cowichan River with my father well into his seventies, and he finally quit when he could no longer safely negotiate the swim downriver.

Dad spent his early childhood swimming in the Capilano River and English Bay. His early teens had been amazing, as he had been reared by his father, a First World War pilot who had served with the Royal Flying Corps from 1915 to 1918. My grandfather was born in Cardiff, Wales, and I deeply covet my British heritage, as my mother was born in Crawley, Sussex, before coming to Canada in 1946 as a British war bride.

Our father was an exceptional athlete, and he had joined the North Vancouver, Lonsdale Boys Athletic Boxing Club at the age of eight. At the age of fifteen, he worked part-time in a drug store on Lonsdale Avenue that was owned and managed by a Hungarian pharmacist by the name of Bobinski affectionately known by his friends and clients as "Bo"

According to family history, Bo, a former boxing coach in Hungary, managed and trained our father in a boxing ring that he and my father built above the drugstore. Bo trained Dad right up until war broke out in 1939. Dad was an exceptional boxer, and he competed in the 1938 Junior Olympics Boxing Venue.

Our father continued boxing during his incarceration in the prison camps, and as a result of his exceptional boxing skills, he was able to escape five times. I proudly display his prison camp fight cards from the stalags that he was interned in between 1942 and 1945.

In 1951, my father became active as a union representative, and the following year was elected president of the Local 180 Union of the International Woodworkers of America. I recall being a small boy and going into the Chinese Village at Ashburnham Creek in Honeymoon Bay with my father. The small Chinese community resided in converted railway cars, and I remember the woodstoves and the piles of mill "tail ends" they used for heating their make-shift homes.

My father was well respected by the Chinese workers, and we often spent Christmas visiting them in their homes. I remember going into the converted boxcars, where the rooms were partitioned by gray wool blankets. A hot wood-stove heated the interior, and there was very little furniture.

One particular Christmas, my father took me to visit one his Chinese friends, and seeing that I was feeling shy, one of the ladies offered me a lychee nut, a rare Chinese delicacy. For years, I recall visiting the Chinese village and growing respectful of the difference in cultures. My father told me that a Chinese friend was a friend for life.

When I was six years old, my father started the Honeymoon Bay Boxing Club in the old Mill Cookhouse, where I had the good fortune to box and train. As a result of the skills he passed on to me, I continued boxing until I was in my early thirties. My father and I shared a strong bond, and he made me proud to learn the science of pugilism; I was taught to box under the Marquess of Queensberry Rules. He also taught me not to be a bully, which became a well-known fact in the schools that I attended, as I was known to be a defender of the weaker and more vulnerable boys.

After living on the lake for nearly nine years, my family and I moved to a rental house in Duncan. Having met Buckshot several months after moving to our newly constructed home on Beverly Street, my life changed significantly. Our new home was across the road from Somenos Creek, a small, fast-moving stream that emptied out of Somenos Lake and paralleled the Trans-Canada Highway, meandering through the Cowichan Tribes Reserve and eventually pouring into Cowichan Bay.

For years, Buckshot and I carried our fishing poles and small pup tent across the field from my house and set up camp on the gently sloped and treed creek bed.

The water was fast-moving, and the current swirled the reeds and bulrushes where the beautifully colored cutthroat trout rested, slowly moving their fins in the current. It was a place where we could cast our line and be assured of a good catch and dinner cooked on an open campfire.

Upon arriving at the creek, we would dig a pit in the ground, lay a small fire on damp rocks taken from the creek, and then bury a large cooking pot full of deep-browned baked beans in anticipation of having a fish and beans dinner.

Having prepared our buried fire and casting our lines into the swiftly running creek, we would soon hook a fat cutthroat trout, playing the twisting and tugging fish over to the bank and flinging it onto the grass. After cleaning the fish, we would ready our cooking fire and fry up the trout, serving it with steaming hot beans.

Cutthroat trout are a type of freshwater salmon species native to the cold-water tributaries of the Pacific Ocean. The meat is pink-colored and very succulent. Adult fish weigh anywhere from one to four pounds, and they are fierce fighters, especially when caught on a juicy worm.

On one such fishing excursion, Buckshot set the pup tent up in the tall grass about thirty feet from the creek as we prepared for the excitement of fishing.

It was early August, and my hay fever was unbearable. My eyes were red and itchy, watering constantly, and my nose ran like a faucet. My incessant sniffling seemed to be annoying the calm and ever-serene Buckshot. At bedtime, we crawled into the tiny two-man pup tent, and lying side by side in our individual sleeping bags, we shared the day's adventures.

During hay fever season, I usually carried a small roll of toilet paper in my shoulder bag as a means of combating the allergies and avoiding Buckshot's ire over my constant sniffling. Turning onto my side to go to sleep, I placed the roll of toilet paper beside my knapsack. Several minutes later, in the cool and quiet evening, Buckshot reached over, grabbed my toilet paper roll, tore off a handful of paper, and said, "One more snort and I am going to shove this roll up your nose."

We roared with laughter, although I knew that he was serious. It was a long and sleepless night as I valiantly attempted to keep myself from sneezing, snorting, and sniffling. Buckshot, a person afflicted with his own special brand of snoring, appeared to get a good night's sleep. However, I must say in retrospect: Buckshot had the patience of Job, and although aware of my discomfort, he generally understood.

As a point of interest, several years after meeting Buckshot, I learned that he had been born deaf in his left ear. Having that knowledge, I was able to position myself on his left side during my bouts of hay fever. In fact, years later, after having spent over twelve years on navy warships and experiencing hearing loss in my right ear from my duty on the deck guns, Buckshot and I would position ourselves so that our hearing loss was on opposite sides. As long as Buckshot drove the vehicle and I was in the passenger seat, we could have a normal conversation.

However, if I was driving, it was impossible to know what the other person was saying. In fact, it became a standing joke that if we were annoyed with each other, we would merely change positions. There were times, however, when we repeated ourselves, which must have seemed odd to other people in our immediate proximity.

Speaking of our mutual hearing loss, I'm reminded during a much later incident, when we were hunting on Buckshot's island. We decided to take his Boston Whaler over to East Thurlow and get a deer.

As we rounded the front of his island and started chugging north in his Boston Whaler, I saw a deer standing on a ledge about a hundred feet above the beach. I was sitting in the bow of the boat, and Buckshot was operating the motor at the stern.

In my excitement, and pointing my hand over his head, I yelled, "Look at the size of that buck!" He turned his head, exposing his good ear in my direction, and while he was looking at the deer on the ledge, I jacked a round into my Browning .308 lever-action rifle and fired off a quick shot. The look on his face was quite odd, although he kept staring up at the rocks; to my utter surprise, the buck leapt in the air, seemed to float off his feet, and then slowly turned backwards and gracefully rolled down to the rocks and onto the beach.

Seeing the deer on the rocks, I yelled at Buckshot to beach the boat so we could field dress the buck. However, he seemed preoccupied with staring at the beach. It was not until much later that Buckshot spoke in an unusually load voice as he mumbled, "Don't mean to ignore you, but I'm just getting the hearing back in my good ear. For a while there, I was completely deaf, and I realized how fortunate I am to have had one good ear."

Realizing what I had unintentionally done, I was absolutely mortified, and I kept apologizing for my lack of consideration and stupidity; however, I don't think Buckshot heard my apology, as he continued shaking his head with a dazed look on his face.

Fishing and hunting with Buckshot was always an adventure, as he was an incredibly skilled and knowledgeable woodsman. His survival skills were legendary in the scouting movement and later as a self-employed gyppo logger. He could exist for days in the wilderness with nothing but a compass, fishhook, piece of string, a knife, and coil of rope.

Returning to the memories of Somenos Creek and having spent the night in the pup tent, we stirred from our sleeping bags and set about building a fire for breakfast. A swim in the creek followed by vigorously brushing our teeth got us ready for the day. After a delightful breakfast of eggs and bacon, Buckshot posed that we were going to spend the morning on Somenos Lake.

Digging through his backpack, Buckshot extracted two large gunnysacks. Not knowing what they were for, I absentmindedly asked, "Where did you get those, and what are they for?"

Looking at me strangely he replied, "We're going to hustle over to the other side of the creek, build a raft, paddle out onto the lake, and catch us a few sacks full of catfish."

Not wanting to appear like a dumb younger kid, I nodded as if I knew exactly what he was talking about. "Sure, Buckshot, catfish . . . yeah—great idea," was my half-hearted response.

Going over the bridge on Lakes Road, we hiked along the creek bank to the place where the Garry Oak trees grew in a field above the creek, and where the creek came out of the lake. Scrounging logs and trees, Buckshot produced a long length of rope, and with lashing knots he secured the logs together. Being a good swimmer was not a problem; however, keeping the makeshift craft together proved to be a challenge. Polling off the bank, we pushed our way into the small and heavy foliaged lake.

While fishing the bottom for catfish, I made a promise to get a small tin boat that we could drag over to the creek. Several hours later, with the two gunnysacks filled with slimy catfish, we trudged down Beverly Street to the Chinese Village located in downtown Duncan.

In 1959, Chinatown was located where the Duncan Courthouse and Round Building are now situated. The Chinese community buildings consisted of a large, 1930s wooden hotel on either end of the block with a long community cookhouse joining the two outer buildings. There were approximately ten steps, each

fifty feet wide, going up and into the community cookhouse.

Dragging our two wet gunnysacks up the
stairs, Buckshot admonished me to keep my
mouth shut during the negotiations. Reaching
the top of the stairs, I looked at the elderly
Chinese men sitting on the front porch of the
huge weather-beaten building. Inside, a singsong cadence of Chinese dialogue permeated
the mysterious dining hall. Hundreds of Chinese
men shuffled around in black two-piece *Mao Tse
Tung* suits with a single pigtail hanging down
their backs. These men were much different
from our Chinese friends in Ashburnham creek.

Most of the males in the Chinese Village wore
long "Fu Manchu–style" chin whiskers, and upon
seeing two boys dragging gunnysacks into the
kitchen, several of the cooks gathered around
while a huge and daunting head cook, dressed
in dirty whites and weighing about three hundred
pounds, strode towards us waving a meat cleaver
in the air. As a twelve-year-old boy, I was totally
mesmerized by his size and demeanor and
feared that I would never see my family again.

Buckshot turned his head towards me and
whispered, "Remember, Johnnycakes, keep
quiet and listen to what I say."

Utterly transfixed, I watched my older companion play the head cook like a four-stringed
Chinese lute. With a sudden darting motion, not

expected of a man his size, the cook grabbed the gunnysack from my hands and spilled the contents onto the floor.

Suddenly, thirty or forty Chinese men, who had been eating their lunch in the cookhouse, jumped from their seats and started yammering at the sight of the slimy and bewhiskered fish.

Several more people came out of the kitchen as the head cook and his minions began shaking the catfish and looking at Buckshot for a price. With a knowing smile, Buckshot gave me one last warning glance and said, "Three dollars for sack, no penny less." Buckshot then hefted one of the sacks, shook it in the air, lowered it down to the floor, and turning down the sides of the gunnysack, he began rooting for the biggest fish.

To our disgust, the boss cook sprayed spittle in our faces as he excitedly shook a catfish in each hand. "2 dolla and not a penny more," he hissed at Buckshot, who shook his head and grabbed another two-pound catfish from the slimy sack. Shaking the fish in the air, he replied, "Big fish, feed lots of people. You make big money selling in cookhouse."

There was another hissing expostulation as the boss cook said, among the wailing of the other cookhouse patrons, "You bad boy alla time bring fish and want more money. Two dolla fifty cents, no more."

With a contented smile, Buckshot turned towards me and said to the boss cook, "Okay, good deal, five dollars for both sacks."

Within seconds, the fish disappeared into the kitchen, and in stunned silence we watched the cooks whacking the fish into little pieces and tossing them into a huge pot of boiling water sitting on the large wood-burning stove. Taking our five dollars, we raced off down the stairs laughing with delight at having sold the two sacks of fish. As we headed for the Totem Café on the corner of Jubilee and Government Streets, across from the Chinese village, we excitedly talked about buying a well-earned hamburger and French fries.

For the next two years, Buckshot and I sold catfish to the Chinese Cookhouse, which greatly enhanced our cash flow. Sometime in the early 1970s, Chinatown was torn down so that a new Provincial Courthouse and office spaces could be erected at the location. The Chinatown buildings were moved to Whippletree Junction, where they sit to this day as a local historical monument.

***

When not fishing, we spent considerable time in the trees at the rear of Buckshot's property, playing with the antique cars and feeding his rabbits. Buckshot had a small black cocker spaniel that always seemed to be tugging at our heels. His name was Poncho, and he followed us everywhere we went. He was a curly little cute dog, and I knew that Buckshot was very fond of him, although he generally slept outside in the backyard. Poncho loved going fishing, and he would waddle along behind us as we headed towards the creek.

Sometimes Poncho would disappear, and I became overly concerned that he would get lost. However, Buckshot would respond to my concerns with, "He's a dog; don't worry, he can look after himself." I never did understand his thinking about the dog, as I had been raised believing that animals were house pets and depended on us for their survival and care. There were times when Poncho would wait for hours at the front door of the old mansion looking for the two of us to come out of the root cellar. Looking back on it now, I can honestly say that Poncho was well fed and always had a black glossy coat.

Chapter 3
The Scouting Years

The scouting years with Buckshot and Second Duncan Troop between 1958 and 1964 were some of the happiest years of my childhood. Buckshot was very close to my father, who had earned the respect of every teenage boy in the community. Dad was an exceptional parent, teacher, and role model—something he learned from being raised by a British Royal Flying Corps officer and gentleman. There were occasions; however, when I felt a small twinge of jealousy with my scouting companions, as I found it difficult sharing my father with the other boys. My dad knew this, and in an attempt to make a man of me, he would center me out as a discipline example for the others—something that I did not really appreciate until many years later, when I made the Royal Canadian Navy a career.

As Buckshot was one of the Senior Scouts in the troop, I stuck close to him during our early scouting activities. He was promoted to Patrol Leader of the Eagle Patrol in early 1960, and through his leadership and friendship, I became the Patrol Leader of the Owl Patrol. Because there were four patrols in the troop, the competition to be the best patrol was invigorating, and it encouraged *esprit de corps*.

In the summer of 1959, my father and his friend Mr. Arnold, a former Olympic swimmer, arranged for a series of Royal Life-Saving Swimming Camps at nearby Shawnigan Lake. Together they organized three consecutive summers of swim camps. We started out as juniors and graduated as Bronze Medallion Lifeguards. I was the only boy in the troop to be hired as the first lifeguard at Maple Bay, a beautiful beach on the inland waters of Vancouver Island. I recall that the British Columbia Forest Products (BCFP) Pulp Mill had built me a tenfoot high lifeguard tower, which sat on the beach near the concrete stairs accessing the beach from the upper parking lot.

As a sixteen-year-old boy, I perched on the railing of the stand, diligently watching over hundreds of local swimmers enjoying the inland waters of the Pacific Ocean.

During one of the summer swim camps, we set up our troop near the Catholic school on the east side of the lake. Unknown to us senior boys, the school was being used that summer as a shelter for a group of delinquent teenage girls.

At the first campfire of the training session, my father explained to the troop with a somewhat straight face that the "bad girls" were completely out of bounds, and that we were forbidden to "fraternize" with the girls, and anyone caught near the girls would be severely punished and most likely sent home. The threat seemed to fall on deaf ears, as several of the senior boys grinned and lowered their heads. Now, it is interesting to say, in retrospect, that it is really foolish to tell teenage boys that "bad girls" are out of bounds.

For the next few days, five of us senior lads did our best to make contact with the bad girls; however, the Sisters of the Church were very vigilant in their scrutiny of the girls.

On the first Saturday night of the swimming camp, my father decided that he was going to allow a group campfire, so that the Sisters and their wards could see how a ceremonial campfire was officially conducted. With a murmur of excitement, Buckshot and I prepared the campfire for the ceremony. We set up long wooden benches in a horseshoe shape, built the ceremonial campfire, and readied ourselves for the first encounter.

At around 7:00 p.m. on that fateful night, the young ladies and the Sisters entered the campfire circle and sat on the opposite side from the troop. About six of us older boys immediately pinged on the chosen beauty of our daydreams and began a campaign of flirting in an effort to gain favour and attention. During the ceremony, we sang songs, acted out skits, and generally amused our guests about the virtues of scouting.

As the evening drew to a close, Dad, the Scoutmaster, announced that the young ladies would leave first and then the Scouts would depart to their campsites, starting with the youngest boys. I think his plan was designed to ensure that the older boys would still be at the campfire by the time the "bad girls" were safely tucked away in the school dormitory.

Ah, young teenage boys are ever-industrious, and during the twilight singing we were able to convey that five or six of us would meet the more senior young ladies by the boathouse later that evening.

As fate would have it, Buckshot and I were able to veer away from our campsite, and in the dark we made our way to the boathouse. To our utter joy, there, at the boathouse, four or five young ladies were waiting as anticipated. Thinking that we had a few hours, we decided to have a swim, and while thrashing in the water with our new friends, we heard an authoritative voice from the darkness order us out of the water. Everyone scattered, and I, the Scoutmaster's son, froze in place.

Standing before me as I dripped in my wet clothes were my father and the Head Sister. Buckshot, a true buddy to the very end, was hiding in the bushes and whispering for me to "quickly run away." Unfortunately, I was transfixed by the glare of my father and the wringing of the Head Sister's hands. I remember my father groaning and telling me that he was very disappointed in me, and that I was to immediately return to my tent, and that he would deal with me later. In utter shame and disgrace, I trudged head down towards my campsite.

Seconds later, Buckshot edged out from the bushes and said, "Johnnycakes, just say nothing." In forlorn despair, I saw my scouting career in shambles.

Sleeping that night was next to impossible, as I had some idea of the wrath that would follow me in the morning. Sure enough, after the morning flag raising ceremony, my father, who had not looked at me since the night before, advised that a court of honor would be convened immediately after the troop was dismissed for swimming lessons.

A court of honor is the authority for discipline matters of the entire troop, and the court members comprise the Troop Leader, Patrol Leaders, and Scoutmaster. Our court of honor consisted of the Troop Leader, Buckshot, three other Patrol Leaders (one of which should have been me), and my father, who was the presiding officer of the court.

Now, the seventeen-year-old Troop Leader did not particularly like me, as I was the Scoutmaster's son, and he being the eldest and most senior boy in the troop, greatly envied my relationship with the Scoutmaster. In addition, the Troop Leader was the senior chair of the court and his word was revered by my father.

Convened in the Scoutmaster's tent, the trial began. Father read out the charges and directed that the court of honor weigh all the facts, hear the evidence, and make a ruling in that regard. He further stated that he would then pronounce a sentence based on the recommendations of the court.

Having heard Buckshot's warning in the bushes the night before, I decided to say nothing in my defense. Well, within ten minutes, the Troop Leader had, with great relish, proclaimed me guilty of horrible sins and recommended that I be demoted as a Patrol Leader and sent home. With a catch in his voice, my father ordered me to stand before the court and "accept [my] punishment."

Upon hearing the verdict of the court, I could see the anguish and obvious humiliation in my father's eyes. However, before I could stand and be made an example to the others, Buckshot leapt to his feet, and in obvious defiance of the Troop Leader and my father's imminent punishment, he blurted, "Sir, if Johnnycakes is stripped of his rank and sent home, then the entire court of honor, including the Troop Leader, Patrol Leaders, and myself should also be stripped of our rank and sent home."

My father was horrified at the audacity of Buckshot, and he demanded an explanation. Buckshot looked around the tent, and staring into the eyes of each and every one of my peers, said that all five of the boys, including himself, had been swimming with the girls, and that I, Johnnycakes, was the only one who had not run and consequently been caught.

The faces of my peers turned red as the Troop Leader and Patrol Leaders bowed their heads. With a slight smile on his face, my father stood up from his chair, cleared his throat, and announced, "Having heard the testimony of the senior Patrol Leader and the culpability of the court of honor, it is not in the best interest of the troop and the lifesaving camp to send the Senior Leaders home. The matter is closed."

Buckshot was my hero, and the indiscretion was never mentioned again, except in the company of my best pal, who knew from the start that my father would not jeopardize the swimming camp by sending all the senior boys home. Buckshot was indeed a loyal and calculating chap.

***

Between mid-November 1960 and New Years of 1961, it rained for more than six weeks straight. The Somenos Creek, directly across from our home flooded over the road and water came halfway up our front lawn. For several days, in anticipation of the early January high tide at Cowichan Bay, we put all our furniture and belongings up on blocks for fear of the water coming into the house.

To our horror, in the early morning hours of January 3, the water began coming inside the house. By mid-morning, we had more than six inches of water on our floors with more water expected at full tide at midnight, and we had no other choice but to evacuate. Standing up to my waist in the water on the street in front of our home, I could see that the subdivision was completely flooded. While waiting for my father to form a plan of evacuation, I heard someone yelling from the far end the street. Looking towards the highway, I saw Buckshot standing in a small tin boat, pushing his way towards our home. He rowed into our driveway and secured the boat by our carport door.

For the rest of the day and far into the night, Buckshot transported most of the sub-division families out of their homes. My father was delighted to see him, and I spent the next six weeks living at his house, as my parents and family were billeted out. As a Scout, Buckshot was always prepared and put others first.

Our scouting adventures were endless. We ran blood donor clinics, attended camporees and jamborees all over Canada, and spent endless days earning merit badges. By the time he was fifteen, Buckshot had earned twenty-one merit badges, and by the time he was seventeen he proudly wore his gold All Around Cord and Bushman's Thong. He was an inspiration to me, and for every badge or award he earned, I was right behind him. He inspired me and I rose to the challenge and became a better Scout.

After school, Buckshot would often ride over to our house and lay out a plan for a new merit badge. It was fun, and we spent months working on getting more and more badges. Some of the badges that we earned were relative to our activities. For example, Buckshot wanted to buy some chickens, so he studies for his poultry badge. Looking after Poncho, his little black dog, earned him his pet keeper's badge, although I did remark to him that Poncho generally took care of himself. The list of badges was endless, and we continued adding them to the sleeves of our Scout uniform. Taking a first aid course earned another badge, and searching for First Nation middens and relics earned us our Pathfinder Badge.

Thinking of ways to earn more badges, we hatched a plan to build a scout shed in my backyard. Father was pleased with our initiative, and we started construction of the ten-by-ten-square-foot hut. It turned into a work of art, and Dad brought home four-by-eight-sheets of heavy kraft pulp paper, which we used to cover the walls after stuffing newspaper between the studs. The scout shed turned into a major building project, and soon we were living in the shed most weekends. We bought a used set of weight-lifting equipment at a garage sale and spent our evenings pumping weights. Being dedicated and trustworthy Scouts, our families respected our privacy and the "scout shed" became our second home—hence the Carpentry and Housekeeping badges we earned.

We painted the outside of the scout shed red and put a lock on the door. The two windows had dark-out curtains, and our privacy was assured for the activities that teenage boys like to manifest.

In fact, I think we had our first bottle of beer in the scout shed at around the age of fifteen. My father suspected that fact, and when he asked me if we were drinking in the shed, I replied, "Once in a while." My father was very trusting of me, because he knew that I would always tell him the truth regardless of the consequences. It was a good feeling, and if I got into a position whereby my veracity was challenged, I merely needed to say to my father, "Scout's Honor" and the matter was permanently closed. We maintained that relationship for the rest of his life.

Every Scout who desired to become a Queen's Scout was required to earn a Second Class Badge, First Class Badge, and five mandatory proficiency badges in addition to taking a First Class Journey. Buckshot took me on his First Class Journey on Saltspring Island in 1961.

We left Duncan on our bicycles at 0700 hours on a wet and miserable Saturday morning in late November. We rode our heavily laden bikes over twenty-six miles, crossing on a ferry from Crofton to Vesuvius Bay and then riding another fourteen miles; where we opened a sealed envelope at a designated place, directing that we proceed to a site at Fulford Harbour near Burgoyne Bay. We mapped and charted the entire journey, and I still have my handwritten logs.

On my First Class Journey, Buckshot volunteered to send me a Morse code message on the Saturday night from Vancouver Island to Salt

Spring Island as a requirement of my badge. The success of the journey was contingent on following sealed orders, setting up camp, cooking a full-course meal for an instructor, and correctly recording a signal message that would be sent from the Crofton Wharf. My journey was in late October of 1962, and it was a particularly wet and miserable weekend. I was accompanied by a Junior Scout, so that he in turn could learn how to complete his First Class Journey if he were to qualify as a Second Class Scout.

On my particular journey, Buckshot asked my mother, a Cub Leader in the same group as my father, to drive him to the Crofton wharf so that he could send me the message from a Second World War Navy signal lamp.

The lamp was encased in a black wooden box with the round single scope-like light attached to a battery. As I waited in the dark on the beach that wet and miserable night at the designated place at 2000 hours, it was impossible to distinguish the ferry traffic headlights from the signal lamp being operated by Buckshot. The distance was about three miles across the bay, and I felt sinking despair, knowing that if I did not record the correct message, I would fail my First Class Journey and disappoint my father and Buckshot.

After about forty-five minutes of waiting in the dark and my companion annotating what we believed was a message from Buckshot, I felt that the journey was over and my chances of earning my First Class Badge were now history. In despair, and just as we were leaving to go back to our soggy bivouac, I heard a noise in the bay across from the beach. Not knowing what was happening, we walked down to the shore, and there in a small boat about two hundred yards out in the bay was Buckshot.

Over the sound of the waves and the chilly blowing rain, Buckshot yelled, "The vehicle traffic is really heavy getting on and off the ferry and the headlights from the traffic are interfering with my message. I am going to send you the message from the point."

I was overjoyed, and we both returned to our pre-arranged position. Sure enough, about fifteen minutes later, I saw the welcome flashing of the signal lamp. Within five minutes, I had deciphered the message, which my companion recorded: "It is stated that the Czechoslovakian Empire is in a state of furor." After receiving the message, I flashed the letter "R" the international code for "roger." In addition, I flashed back: "Thanks, Buckshot, I owe you another one."

After getting back home, I learned on the following Monday that Buckshot, out of concern for me, had rented a boat and rowed three miles from Crofton to the point across from my designated location. My mother did not question why he had been gone in the dark and rain for hours sending the message, because she knew that he was a reliable Scout.

***

Sometime in the summer of 1960, Buckshot told me that we should put together an application to attend the Third Canadian Scout Jamboree that was being held in Ottawa, Ontario, the following July. This was a rare opportunity, as the previous Canadian Jamboree had been held in Niagara Falls in 1955. We both agreed that we needed to submit an application and earn some money towards the registration, trip fees, and miscellaneous expenses. After convincing my father and the hierarchy at the Group Committee level, Buckshot and I set about earning the fees for the upcoming event.

On a warm spring afternoon in 1961, Buckshot and I set off on our bicycles on a twenty-six-mile ride to the local sawmill in Youbou, which was operated by British Columbia Forest Products. Off we went, departing at daybreak, knowing that we would have a four-to-five-hour ride on a narrow and dangerous back road where huge chipper trucks often roared by, creating a draft that was capable of pulling us off the road.

Every time a large semi-trailer full of wood chips or sawdust went racing by, we wobbled on our bikes and got a face full of sawdust. It was very dangerous, and Buckshot and I would fling ourselves in the ditch and comment on the "close call." The ride was generally fun, and we stopped and ate our bag lunch in Lake Cowichan for a few minutes before jumping back on our bikes and heading out on the last leg of the journey.

Arriving at the Personnel Office shortly before noon, we signed up as weekend cleanup crew, earning $1.68 per hour. The work was dirty, difficult, and backbreaking, and Buckshot was still working at the local Safeway grocery store after school. However, having the summer off meant he could work two jobs to earn some money for the Jamboree.

At that time, I was delivering newspapers and working as a pinsetter at the Duncan Bowling Alley on Tuesday and Thursday evenings, so weekend work would not pose a problem for me.

After a few weeks doing cleanup in the gang mill, I was sent to the mill garage and given a plum job washing lumber carriers, boom boats, and other vehicles. It was fun working alone in the garage, as the master mechanic and his helper worked Monday to Friday.

The routine was that Buckshot and I would carpool with the shift workers who worked on Saturday and Sunday. Arriving at the mill, we would go our separate ways, and then ride back home together after work.

The garage where I worked was a large building a considerable distance from the main mill and lake. After changing into my coveralls, I would read the instructions on the chalkboard hanging on the shop wall. On one particular Saturday morning, the Master Mechanic had written on the blackboard that I was to clean the grease and oil off the engine in *Lulu*, the twenty-foot tug boat tied up on the outer boom, then drive *Lulu* to the boat ramp for pickup by the second mechanic on the following Monday morning.

As I proceeded to the lake and log booms, I spotted Buckshot working under a catwalk with a shovel and wheelbarrow. He did not appear overjoyed shoveling pieces of wet and smelly bark, and he asked me what I was doing away from the garage. With a smug look on my face, I told Buckshot what I was going to do with *Lulu*.

With an interesting smile, he replied, "Wow, let's flash her up and take a spin around the lake. No one's around, and it should be fun."

Well, something in my spirit told me that I was making a big mistake. Anyhow, considering that Buckshot was an experienced boat handler, I agreed to the challenge.

Stepping gingerly onto the unstable, half-submerged boom logs, we managed to locate

Lulu nesting against the furthest boom, rocking gently to and fro on the calm lake in breezy contentment. Jumping in the solid steel tug, I told Buckshot that I should be the one to drive the boat, as it was my responsibility to take *Lulu* to the boat launch. Buckshot agreed and I flashed up the motor while Buckshot untied the lines.

With eager anticipation, I shoved the throttle stick forward and *Lulu* shot away from the boom. For the next fifteen minutes we raced around the lake, causing a wake that set the string of logs dancing around the booms. Full turns, half turns, and every which way, I pushed *Lulu* through her paces.

Glancing towards shore, I noticed several older men shaking their heads and grinning at us with a knowing look. I yelled over the roar of the tug, "Buckshot, the millwrights are watching us. I'd better let you off on the closest boom so you won't get in trouble with your charge-hand."

Buckshot grunted something as I cranked over the helm, headed towards the boom, hauled *Lulu* up short in a wake of spraying water, and smoothly glided alongside a big boom stick. Buckshot jumped onto the log and headed back to the gang mill, appearing to be impressed with my newfound seamanship skills.

Feeling like a bit more excitement, I raced *Lulu* out past the log booms, opened the throttle full ahead, and spun her in a full curve towards the shore ramp. Running along at a pretty good clip, I realized that something was wrong with *Lulu*'s steerage, and it fleetingly occurred to me that maybe the throttle linkage was the reason *Lulu* was being hauled ashore for repairs.

Not being an experienced boom boat operator, and going way too fast for the amount of distance to the shore, I made a decision to run *Lulu* up on a boom log in an effort to reduce speed so that I could slow her down and get her safely to the launch.

Glancing towards the boom, I saw Buckshot shaking his head as he tried to warn me of the fate that seemed obvious to everyone but me. With a sudden panic rising in my chest, I tried to slow *Lulu* down as she hit the log square on. The next thing I knew, *Lulu* was airborne and flying over the log, while I was trying to keep her from tearing off the propeller. As anticipated by everyone but me, *Lulu* shot over the log and took a nosedive into the lake. The last thing I remembered was jumping over the side as *Lulu* sank headfirst in about ten feet of water.

Swimming towards the boom, I heard a gurgling sound as *Lulu*'s diesel engine choked out and she sank beneath the surface. In utter disbelief, I crawled up on the rolling and twisting boom, lurched back to shore, and stared with an open mouth where *Lulu* should have been resting at the boat launch.

I heard Buckshot yelling above the laughing of the older guys, "Good ride, Johnnycakes, let's hope you still have a job on Monday."

In utter humiliation, I trudged back to the garage in my soaking overalls and wet squishing work boots. On the way back to the garage, I racked my brain as to how I was going to explain *Lulu* sitting on the bottom of the lake, two days before her scheduled repairs.

I didn't lose my job, but unfortunately, that was not the last misjudgment I made while working at the mill. Six months later, on a cold and snowy December morning, I turned over a Ross lumber carrier on the railway tracks while joyriding from the gang mill to the garage.

On both those occasions, the master mechanic admonished me for being a "hotshot kid." He must have liked me, because I still had my job and was working in anticipation of acquiring an apprenticeship.

Having saved some money from the job working in the Youbou mill and our other part-time jobs, Buckshot and I were able to pay some monies towards the cost of the Jamboree. My father was pleased with us, as we also had some spending money for the trip.

On a sunny morning in late July, 1961, Buckshot and I set off from the Duncan bus depot loaded with packsacks full of scouting gear with other scouts from Chemainus, Lake Cowichan, Cobble Hill, Mill Bay, and Victoria. We received a hearty wave goodbye from the parents and Scout Leaders.

We rode north to Nanaimo by Coach Lines, took the Black Ball Ferry across to Vancouver, and then caught a passenger train for Ottawa, Ontario, arriving five days later at the Connaught Mountain Range Scout Camp. Over the next few days, we were joined by thousands of other Scouts from all across Canada.

The Jamboree was an incredible experience whereby we were engaged in every type of scouting activity possible from early in the morning until late at night. Every troop was designated an area to set up their camp. Fortunately, Buckshot and I were together in the British Columbia Contingent.

The program was vigorous, and there was not much free time, as there were voluntary and mandatory activities. One of the voluntary activities was boxing, and Buckshot encouraged me to sign up for the bouts. I agreed on the condition that he would act as my second, and I soon entered the boxing competitions.

I did well in the first four fights and progressed to the semifinals, eventually earning my way to the finals. It was then that I learned I would be competing against a Scout from the

Oak Bay Troop in Victoria. This was a comfort, as we would be representing all the Scouts from Vancouver Island.

During the previous bouts, Buckshot, true to his word, had participated as my second. As was customary, after the bell rang, he would rush into the ring, plunk me down on the stool, and give me a full minute of complex instructions.

Amateur boxing consists of three 3-minute rounds with headgear and a kidney belt. The twelve-ounce gloves are like pillows, and if you miss your target on an overhand right, you generally lose your balance and set yourself up for the dreaded counterpunch.

During the final fight of the boxing venue, Buckshot yelled instructions at me: "Tuck your chin! Raise your hands! Dance to the right, jab with the left, shift your feet, and follow up with a right cross!" I danced around the ring in pursuit of my opponent.

According to Buckshot, round one appeared even. After round two, Buckshot nodded that I had won the round, and sitting on the stool before the final bell for the last three minutes of slugging and grunting, Buckshot whispered, "He's tiring, Johnnycakes, now is the time to move in and overwhelm him with combinations, as I think you've got a round each on the score cards."

As anticipated (and way too soon), the final bell rang, and off I charged while Buckshot yanked my stool out of the square ring. Circling my opponent, whom I considered a friend and fellow Scout, the opponent whispered, "Take it easy, buddy, your punches are really hurting, and this is only for fun."

Well, being a sucker for punishment, I stepped back, paused, and nodded my head in acknowledgement of the considerate comment.

Dropping my guard, I heard Buckshot yelling behind me that I was being set up and to protect myself at all times. With my hands partially down, the wily opponent let go a flurry of punches, staggering me back so that my hands fell to my sides. With about ten seconds left before the final bell and the ominous end at hand, I rushed forward and caught a right hand square in the face. My knees buckled, but I kept myself upright. With a knowing smile on his face, my sneaky opponent raised his hands above his head in victory as the final bell tolled the end.

Returning to my corner, I noticed that Buckshot had not brought in my stool. Not only was he angry with my less-than-perfect performance, he also expostulated that I had blown the finals. Buckshot later proved to be a fast and hard puncher who could hit like a sledge-hammer. I learned this from being cocky with him in our carport about a year later. In fact, he was one of the strongest men I had ever met, considering his small but compact stature.

***

Arriving back on the Island in the middle of August, Buckshot and I went back to our part-time jobs with renewed vigor. The Jamboree had been a wonderful experience, and our new skills were to greatly enhance our training at the troop level.

Several years after going to the Jamboree in Ottawa, I learned that my "worthy boxing opponent" had turned professional, and that I had unwittingly made it easier for that to happen. However, my father told me that he was pleased with my boxing skills, and that he expected me to turn professional by the time I was nineteen. Unfortunately, a physical injury precluded me from securing a professional boxing career.

The following year, Buckshot and I were chosen to represent the Vancouver Island Scout Marathon in recognition of the Centennial Celebration for the City of Victoria. Our task was to pass over the Centennial greeting scroll that originated in Campbell River and was being relayed 150 miles south to our provincial capital named after Queen Victoria. It was a special occasion, and Buckshot and I were delighted to have been chosen to deliver the scroll by bicycle from Duncan City Hall to the top of the Malahat Drive, a distance of about twenty miles, the last six miles of which were at the top of a 1,100-foot (Malahat) mountain pass.

The scroll was transported from Campbell River, starting on July 28, by bicycle, runner, and horseback, and it was delivered to a luncheon of past and present civic dignitaries on the city's one hundredth birthday. Municipal offices from each of the communities in the relay added congratulatory comments to the scroll. On July 28, Buckshot and I attended Duncan City Hall attired in full Scout uniform, where we officially received the scroll from Cowichan Tribe Chief Mike Underwood and Alderman Rick Cairns, the acting mayor of the City of Duncan. It was an auspicious event, and both Buckshot and I made the local newspaper complete with a photograph.

There were many times when the troop competed in intercommunity scouting activities, whereby we received official awards. Buckshot eventually became the Troop Leader, and his fairness and loyalty made our troop the best in the Valley. My father was very proud of Buckshot, and we both attended Government House a year apart to receive our Queen Scout Awards. Both our homes were filled with pictures of us in full scouting uniforms.

In the spring of 1963, my father announced that our Scout Troop was going to build and erect a large, fifteen-foot-high wooden gateway at the bottom of the hiking trail going into Maple Mountain Park.

The gateway was an aggressive project and several senior scouts, including Buckshot and I, had been assigned the project. The task was to locate the trees, assemble the gateway, dig the holes, raise the pillars, and cement the gateway into the ground.

However, before we could start construction on the project, we had to find the right-sized trees and cut them down so we could begin work. As we were pondering the chore, Buckshot stepped forward in front of our group and volunteered, saying, "Finally, I get to do something with trees. I've been waiting for months to cut down some trees on this mountain." We knew at that time that Buckshot was going to take over the project and prove himself a logger.

Several weekends later, the project was finished, and during an official opening ceremony the local newspaper took photographs of the Scouts standing under the majestic archway. At the top of the arch, we had burned in the name and details of the gateway.

In the summer of 1963, I quit my job at Youbou Sawmill and started working at the MacMillan Bloedell Sawmill in Chemainus. Chemainus was much closer to home, and the rising cost of gasoline made it easier to make the decision.

In the winter of 1963, through the natural progression of leadership, I became the Troop Leader, as Buckshot had left the scout troop and started working full-time in the logging Industry. He would be eighteen the following May, and his leaving six months early made it possible for me to step into the coveted position.

It felt strange not having him in the troop, so I focused my energy on passing on my skills to the younger boys. However, I was—and forever will be—grateful to Buckshot for teaching me how to survive in the woods, manoeuver fishing boats, and in particular, to live in the moment. He always focused on the task at hand and the people immediately in his company; furthermore, he was easygoing and always ready to find the humor in most situations. Although he was a strong and capable man, he enjoyed a friendly game of cards and a few laps in his pool. His spontaneous nature was infectious, and he was delightful to be around. I truly envied his laid-back nature.

Immersing fully into the responsibilities of being the Troop Leader was a very rewarding and educational experience. Both of the Assistant Scoutmasters were supportive of my role, as they had younger boys of their own in the troop who relied heavily on my seniority and experience. For the next year, I participated in numerous scouting activities: camporees, jamborees, and community rallies.

It was difficult at times, as I did not have Buckshot there to share the program with.

However, the training was most valuable, and years later, while serving in the military, I started my own Scout Troop while stationed at Camp Borden, Ontario.

When I was the Scoutmaster of the Second Borden Scout Troop, the chairman of the Group Committee was an Army Captain who happened to be my immediate superior at the Canadian Forces School of Medical Services. He was the Adjutant of the school, and the School Commandant was a four-ringed Navy Captain whose twelve-year-old son was in my Troop; this was a definite benefit to my status in the training Unit.

During a cold and wintery day in early January, I told the troop that we were going to gear up for a winter survival camp. The boys were relatively young as it was a new troop, and there was immediate sense of excitement.

At the Wednesday evening troop meeting before the coming weekend event, I instructed the lads to write down a list of provisions that they would need for the week-end training exercise.

I explained that the purpose of the camp was to be totally self-reliant—we would live off the land—and that they were going to be taught how to survive with bivouac shelters, reflector fires, and tinfoil cooking. Boiling snow, sleeping on a cedar bed of boughs, and catching winter trout were some of the program teachings. These were things that Buckshot and I had been doing since we were eleven-year-old Scouts.

At around 1:30 p.m. on the Friday afternoon before setting out on the weekend camp, a ten-ton canvas-covered military truck drove up to the front entrance of the school, and an army corporal came into the building and asked for me by name. In absolute confusion, I met with the corporal, whereby he preceded to hand me a clipboard with about ten pages of items that required my signature. Realizing what was happening, I asked the corporal who had ordered the $20,000 worth of field equipment.

The army truck was filled to the brim with huge wall tents, cots, sleeping bags, and a field kitchen complete with pots, pans, and eating utensils. There was also a two-man team of military cooks assigned to operate the ghastly field kitchen. The corporal immediately advised me that the Adjutant, who happened to be the chair of the Scout Group Committee, had ordered the equipment.

Without further ado, I sent the corporal and his truck away and went back to my desk. Several minutes later, the Adjutant, who unfortunately was my boss, strode into my office, bellowed like a bull elephant, and ordered me into the Commandant's office. I was undaunted; the

Commandant was the senior psychiatrist in the Canadian Forces Medical Services, and he was also the proud father of one of my scouts.

Standing before the Commandant, the Army Captain proceeded to advise the ranking officer that I had directly disobeyed his orders and sent the truck and field supplies away, thereby embarrassing the troop and the Adjutant.

In exasperation, the four-ringed Navy officer—who secretly enjoyed the fact that I was also one of four other Navy-types in the army school—looked at me, and in a bemused voice enquired, "Is it true, Master Seaman, that you sent the supply truck away?"

"Yes, sir," I responded with a blank look on my face.

"See? I was right," expostulated the impetuous Adjutant as he itemized the virtues of field kitchens, wall tents, canvas cots, sleeping bags, and military cooks.

The Commandant looked back at me and again asked me the question,

"Would you please explain why you sent the army supply truck away, Master Seaman?"

With the same benign look, I told the Commandant, "Sir, the purpose of the winter survival course is to teach the scouts how to live off the land and survive in the wilderness."

The Commandant looked directly at the Captain, and with the finesse of a senior military psychiatrist, remarked, "Captain, as you well know, my son Ronald is very much looking forward to the winter campout, and I am sure that the Master Seaman is very grateful for your considerations."

With a red face, the Adjutant turned to me and ordered, "I'll see you in my office, Master Seaman, when you are finished with the Commandant."

I knew then that the rest of my posting at the medical school was going to be a difficult tour, despite having the support of the Commandant. The meeting later with the Adjutant was far from pleasant, and he promised to educate me on the protocol with the Commandant, Group Committee, and Scout Troop. What he did not appreciate was that I had learned far more in my fifteen years of scouting than he would learn in his fifteen months as Chairman of the Group.

Sure enough, my next annual assessment had to be rewritten by the Commandant, as the Adjutant carried his wrath to a much higher level. It was not until I was posted out of the unit two years later that the Adjutant grudgingly shook my hand and complimented me on the "fair job" with the Scout Troop.

Of course, the Commandant wrote an exceptional evaluation report with considerable more praise than the Army Captain. Oh well—everyone in the military should know that the Navy has always been considered the Senior Service.

Chapter 4
The Pathfinder Years

During our scouting years, Buckshot and I were mandated to acquire the Pathfinder Badge, which was one of the four requisite Queen-Scout-qualifying badges. The Pathfinder Badge was highly coveted in scouting, and we spent nearly two years researching the history of the Cowichan Valley. In addition to conducting searches in the local museum, historical society, and Cowichan Tribes' history, we scouted for First Nation middens and relics in Maple Bay and the shores along the Cowichan River Estuary—areas that bordered the First Nations Reserve.

Buckshot was a natural in the art of finding historical artifacts. His keen mind and profound knowledge of local history and folklore had been passed down by his parents and grandparents, who had been raised in Cowichan Station, a rustic and former pioneer village southwest of the City of Duncan.

One of the most interesting areas for yielding First Nation middens was on the shores of Maple Bay. Tribal lore told us that approximately two hundred years ago; a warring tribal party invaded the basin at Maple Bay.

The story goes on to say that the invading war canoes of the much-feared Haida Nation had landed on the shores of Maple Bay beach and were planning a raid on the Cowichan Tribes the following morning. Unbeknown to the invaders, a hunter from the Cowichan Tribes spotted the war party and fled back to warn his tribe.

Haida Warriors from the Queen Charlotte Islands were known for their fierce and brutal raids on the other tribes throughout British Columbia, and the violent and brutal way they murdered and pillaged the villages, taking men, women, and children as slaves.

Upon learning of the invasion, and in the early morning on the following day, the Cowichan Tribes sent a young couple out into the bay in a canoe to lure the waiting invading warriors out in the open. The young couple was told to perform a "courtship drum and song" and pretend not to notice the enemy. The young male and his female companion made an imposing sight.

With a whoop and rush, the Haida took to their war canoes virtually unarmed and unsuspecting in a bloodthirsty fever to capture the couple. The Cowichan Tribes then sprung the trap, and all of their heavily armed warriors rushed forward in their war canoes, attacking and overwhelming the invaders. In this rare and decisive victory, the waters of Maple Bay turned red with blood and hundreds of slain warrior bodies were washed up on the shores, resulting in spears, knives, and flint arrowheads being littered across the beach.

After learning of the huge battle from centuries past, Buckshot and I combed the beaches and dug into the high water bank on the point at Maple Bay. The yield was very fruitful, and we dug up hundreds of arrowheads, First Nation middens, and a First Nation skull with an arrow-shaped hole in the top of the cranium. Buckshot suggested that we put the skull in a paper bag and store it in my father's carport shed until we could find out more information. We were positive that the skull was a female First Nation person from hundreds of year ago, as the upper and lower teeth were worn down—what we presumed to be the result of chewing on leather. Buckshot explained that the females of the tribe chewed the hides to make the leather soft for ease of making clothes.

One evening, not long after finding the rare First Nation middens and the human skull, we secured the skull in a paper bag in my father's carport shed. Several days later, my mother was in the shed looking for something on the counter and mistakenly opened the paper bag, looked inside, shrieked, and dropped the skull on the workbench. The story of the skull was related to both of us later by my father.

When we came home later that night, my enraged and terrified English war bride mother demanded that we remove the skull from the property. On the advice of our Scoutmaster—who unfortunately happened to be my father on that occasion—we were ordered to take the skull to the local RCMP detachment; fortunately, we never heard another word from my father or the police about the incident.

For years, Buckshot and I continued searching for local artifacts and became known by our classmates as the "archeologists" of the Cowichan Valley.

Buckshot's home was filled with relics and First Nation artifacts, and we continued searching at Maple Bay, Cowichan Bay, Chemainus, and years later on his island in the Johnstone Straits.

Chapter 5
The Jalopy Years

For as far back as I can remember Buckshot's father collected antique cars. There were always old cars in tents, garages, backyards, and car lots belonging to his family. The first jalopy that Buckshot purchased from his dad was a 1937 Dodge coupe. It was light gray, lowered at the front, boasted sporty tires, and proudly displayed a set of foam dice hanging from the rear-view mirror. The floor stick shift stood even with the front bench seat, and a drilled-out eight ball was screwed to the top of the shifter. Getting five or six teenage kids into the vehicle was a chore, and on many occasions I shifted the gears while Buckshot manipulated the clutch. It proved difficult one night when we had a bet with another "hot-rodder" that we could get thirteen kids into the coupe and drag race a quarter mile. How we managed to see where we were going is a question for the ages. However, we won the bet—although we ended up in the ditch on the Youbou highway.

At the time Buckshot got his '37 Coupe, I was working on buying a 1952 Chevy four-door sedan. It was not as glamorous as Buckshot's hot rod; however, it was "nearly" my first car, and the only means of transportation affordable at the time. As Buckshot spent most of his time at our place during the summer, he was subject to the rules of our home—and, of course, his Scoutmaster.

On a particular summer afternoon in 1962, my father stated that if we wanted to own and operate a vehicle, then we needed to have the ability to insure, maintain, and fuel the car. He admonished us by saying that if we could not afford to put fuel in the vehicle, then the car had to sit in the yard. Well, this did not go over well with Buckshot, as he was very resourceful and independent. Several weeks later, I received a call from Buckshot. He said that he was coming over later that evening, as we were going to a party.

My father was working a graveyard shift at the Crofton Pulp Mill, and he generally slept in the evening until it was time to go to work. At that time, our family owned a 1958 Husky Hillman station wagon, which was always parked under the carport with the back end facing out into the driveway.

On this particular night, Buckshot arrived sometime around 8:30 p.m. and backed his '37 coupe into our small driveway, stopping about six inches from the rear of the Hillman. As I exited the house in anticipation of an outing with Buckshot, I noticed that he had placed a length of rubber hose into the gas tank of Dad's car and was in the process of siphoning gasoline into his jalopy.

"Hey, Buckshot, what are you doing?" I asked with dreaded consternation.

He responded in a soft and barely audible voice, "Borrowing a few gallons of gas from your dad's car. I'll pay him back on payday."

Shaking my head in awe of his boldness, I told him to hurry up so that we could leave.

The following morning, my father came home from work at around 9:30 a.m., about two hours later than usual, and I could hear him admonishing my mother for not filling the car with gas the day before. I awoke to my mother adamantly declaring that she had in fact filled the car with gas. Not pleased, father further stated that on the way to work the previous evening, and while in a pitch-dark and remote area about two miles from the pulp mill, the vehicle had run out of gas. He had had to walk to the mill, and consequently, he had been late for work. He further lamented that after getting off work at 7:00 a.m., he had been required to walk to the nearest gas station, buy a small can of gas, and walk back to the car so that he could get home and to bed after working all night.

In utter despair, I buried my head under the covers and pretended to be asleep because there was absolutely no way that I could ever tell a lie to my father if he were to interrogate me about the family car being empty the night before.

Buckshot apparently realized his mistake and it never happened again—although his Scoutmaster was not compensated the two dollars' worth of gas.

However, I know that Buckshot made up for that indiscretion in later years, as he delivered free firewood to our parent's home.

The following year, I briefly purchased a 1951 lime green Chevy four-door sedan from a neighbor who lived on the street behind our home.

He was an interesting man who had served twenty-five years in the Royal Canadian Navy as an intelligence officer. In those days, we referred to them as "spooks," as they were like ghosts and seldom seen doing their job and, although he liked to tipple beer, I went to school with his daughter and found him to be an interesting character. On the day of solidifying the deal, I happened to be walking his daughter to school when I spotted the lime green beauty sitting in the long grass at the edge of their driveway. Desperately wanting to buy myself a new car—any car, for that matter—and wanting to be like my buddy Buckshot, I zeroed in on the car and immediately forgot about walking his daughter to school. To the annoyance of his daughter, I woke up her father and blurted out that I was very interested in buying the beautiful car reposing in the sun at the edge of his driveway. With a sleepy grin on his face, he told me to see him after school. Rushing back to his house five minutes after the final school bell rang, I noticed that the grass around my intended purchase had been whacked down and the vehicle had been moved to the side of the road. With a quaver in my voice, I posed the question of "How much?"

The dreaded response was, "Twenty-five dollars."

"Yes," I whispered eagerly, and then I raced home to get my hard-earned and long-suffering cash.

On the way to back home to check the status of my money stash, I briefly recalled my father's warning several weeks before my sixteenth birthday: "Son, be patient, and we will find you the right car."

Oh well—I was certain that Dad would appreciate and understand my initiative, as I had in fact found the right car, and Buckshot was not available to help me; so yes, I was convinced that it was a good deal; it was definitely the right color and within my budget.

As both my parents were at work, I located the cash and raced back to my new car. There, standing in the driveway, was my friend's father. He had opened the hood, trunk, and all the doors of the vehicle and was ready to hand over custody of the beloved possession. As I approached the car, I noticed a small wooden crate of bulk oil sitting in the trunk—the type in glass bottles with a metal pour top screwed to the neck of the jar.

Not knowing why there were that many jars in the trunk, I asked the vendor the purpose. His response was that the older straight-six overhead engine models used a "wee bit of oil now and then," and that it was far more cost-effective to carry the bulk oil in the trunk. I was elated by his profound wisdom and grateful for the free oil. As I walked around the front of my nearly new car, he poured a bottle of refined oil into the engine. About half an hour later, with the transaction completed, he handed me the keys, and in eager anticipation, I turned the key in the ignition. Nothing; silence—not even a clicking sound. Not to be daunted, I exited out of the car and looked at the weather-beaten battery under the open hood.

"Ah," he said, "it has been sitting for a few months, and the battery needs a jump start."

We jumped started the battery from his wife's sedan, and the lime green car shuddered to life. Smoke wafted from the shaking tailpipe, and when I tried to shift into gear, the column shifter seemed to be locked. Anticipating my next question, he volunteered, "Sometimes the shift linkage sticks, and you need to tap the lever with a small rock. This is common with the 1951s. Let me show you how to rectify this temporary situation." Taking a good-sized rock in his hand, the previous owner of about thirty minutes ago whacked the steering rod arm with a sharp smack and directed me to "try now."

Climbing back into the vehicle, I noticed, for the first time, that the seats were quite dirty, and upon this comment he told me to put a gray wool blanket over the seat, "like the rest of the cool kids driving '51 Chevs." Undaunted and still in love with my new car, I managed to shift into first gear, and from having gained experience working with *Lulu* the tug boat at the mill, I moved forward, smoke billowing behind me while the car continued to shake as I eased out on the road and waved goodbye to my new friend. Looking back a few seconds later, I saw him quickly departing in his wife's car.

As I wanted to get the feel of my new acqui-sition, I drove the other way around the block, and within five minutes turned into our driveway. Alas, halfway into the driveway, the car shuddered, coughed, and died.

Exiting the vehicle, I noticed bulk oil pouring out the bottom of the engine and onto my father's driveway. With the help of a neighbour we pushed the car onto the street, and I ran back to my new friend's house. Unfortunately, the vendor had just returned from the government liquor store and appeared to be slightly inebriated. When I explained that the car had died in the driveway, he responded with a slight slurring of words that he had already spent the money and there nothing more that he could do for me.

Realizing that I had defied my father's warning, I sat down by the lime green beast and waited for Dad to get home from work. About an hour later, my father drove into the driveway, and getting out of his vehicle, said in a menacing tone, "My boy, I trust that you did not buy that green clunker sitting on the road in front of our house?"

I turned my head away and began the story about my first "good deal."

Father was known on occasion to be a gentleman in spite of being a former Olympic boxer, army commando, and prisoner of war. After calming down, he called me a "blithering idiot" and said that after dinner we would "deal with the lime green fiasco." Sure enough, after supper—during which I surprisingly remained quiet and ate very little—father walked with me to the seller's home, and in very few words, told him (who, by that time, was quite intoxicated) that he had precisely twenty-four hours to remove the vehicle from in front of our home and return the twenty-five dollars. There was no argument, and several months later, my father helped me buy my "real" first car, which was a 1952 Chev that I financed with the British Columbia Forest Products Crofton Community Credit Union. The payments were ninety-six dollars a month, and I was encouraged to work as many hours at the Sawmill as possible.

The next car that I purchased was a brown-and cream-coloured 1957 Chevrolet Bellaire—the envy of my school chums. By this time, Buckshot was driving a 1934 Ford Roadster, and running around in his classic car proved to be lots of fun.

At that time, there were only three police officers in Duncan; one worked the night shift, the other worked the day shift, and the third sometimes manned the office and switched with the other two.

It became a challenge to find out who was on shift, as one of the constables was a six-foot-seven monstrosity whom we adoringly referred to as "Big Jack." One Friday night, Buckshot and

I were cruising around town looking for some excitement when Big Jack pulled us over by the high school.

When Big Jack the Royal Canadian Mounted Police Constable stood beside the driver's door of your vehicle, his Sam Browne boots were just below the window. Leaning in the car he would say, "I know your fathers. Do they know where you are tonight?" The next order was, "Hand me what's left of the six pack of beer on the seat, son." I would then reluctantly hand over the four remaining bottles of beer.

Going back to his police cruiser, we knew that Big Jack was going to mete out his own personal brand of punishment rather than the stiff arm of the law. Loping back from the police car, he asked the dreaded question: "What are you boys doing this Saturday night?"—which happened to be the next day.

"Nothing, sir," was the simultaneous response.

"Good, then I'll see you at the police station at four o'clock tomorrow afternoon when I come on duty." Off he went, looking for more teenage boys to wash the dirty police cars at the detachment on a Saturday night—a special time that was supposed to be reserved for having fun.

Realizing that our favourite constable seemed to be working more and more weekends, we changed our jalopy cruising to Ladysmith and Nanaimo. It turned out bad there as well, as the word soon spread that the Duncan kids were cruising the streets.

***

My next car was a shiny black 1949 Ford Meteor with red leather seats and chrome around the doors and windows. She was a beautiful automobile, and she got the attention of most of the kids in town. One Saturday night, while cruising the main street with my new glass-pack mufflers, I drove past Buckshot driving his Ford Roadster. As we passed in the downtown area, I yelled out the window that there was a big party behind the Red Rooster Café near the Chemainus River. Looking back through the rear-view mirror, I noticed three or four other jalopies following behind Buckshot, who was behind my heap.

Twenty minutes later, there were at least fifteen or twenty jalopies following each other out of town towards the Red Rooster. Pulling into the rural acreage behind the café, we saw dozens of cars parked on lawns, side streets, and in front of the old farmhouse. Music blared from the old mansion, and hundreds of guys and gals surged in and out of the building. We knew everyone, and, off in the corner I spotted some of my classmates. The house was packed, and everyone was talking at the same time. It was delightful, and Buckshot and I grabbed a cool one and caught up on the latest news in town.

Later in the evening, we heard the sound of several Harley-Davidson motorcycles, and to our absolute surprise, we jumped out of the way as two large motorbikes drove through the house, scattering teenagers every which direction. After catching our breath, and in the safety of the next room, we roared with laughter. As the night wore on and the cars kept arriving on the property, it became necessary to get out of there before our vehicles got blocked in by the other cars.

So off we went to Bob's Pool Hall above the movie theater, which my father regularly referred to as a "Den of Iniquity." It was good clean fun, and seldom did anyone get in trouble. Riding around town in our jalopies was a rite of passage, and every Friday and Saturday night kids, for years to come, parked their jalopies in the public square across from the Totem Café. My jalopy had a small container on the console to hold nickels for the jukeboxes that lined the walls of the Totem café.

***

Between 1963 and 1971, I briefly owned a 51 Chev and then a 49 Meteor, 52 Chev, 56 Ford Crown Victoria, 57 Pontiac, 61 Ford Fairlane, 63 Ford Fairlane, 65 Ford Fairlane, 68 Ford Torino, and 1969 Chev. The Crown Victoria was a V8 Flathead motor, and it purred like a kitten.

One Saturday morning in1963, not long after spending a rather stressful night up island avoiding the local authorities, Buckshot called me and asked if I wanted to go Boyles' Auction Yard in downtown Duncan. Back in the early '60s, the auction covered a full city block along Canada Avenue, two blocks north of the train station. The stockyard, coffee shop, and main auction ring were a gathering spot for the locals. My girlfriend at the time worked in the café—a long, narrow building situated right off the side-walk in front of the livestock buildings.

Heading over to meet Buckshot at the auction, I fondly recalled the time I had first gotten my driver's licence and how, after finish-ing a Saturday dayshift at the Youbou Sawmill, I had driven back to Duncan, parked my jalopy at the front of the café, and wearing my hardhat and work clothes, strutted into the café and immediately embarrassed my fifteen-year-old girlfriend.

Of course, I had dyno taped (a hand-held machine that imprinted raised letters on a strip of plastic with a sticky back) my name on a red and white sticker across the front of my safety hat, further adding to her discomfort. For some strange reason, she quit her job several weeks later.

As I approached the auction yard, I saw Buckshot parking a truck across from the main cattle stalls. On this particular morning, the place was full, and the auctioneer had already started his sales spiel—something that I also learned from listening to his spellbinding rapid-fire sales pitch. As I walked into the arena, I could see that the bleachers above the stock pens were full. It was a wonderful small-town gathering, as people had come to see what was on the auction block that day.

Buckshot came up beside me and whispered in my left ear, "I'm looking to buy a Rhode Island Red rooster and a few chickens. Keep your eyes peeled, and tell me if you see anything worth bidding on."

Knowing that Buckshot had a backyard full of rabbit hutches, I could understand his reason for buying chickens at the Saturday auction.

Shortly thereafter, when all the horses, cows, sheep, and goats had gone through the auction block, Buckshot gently nudged me in the ribs and pointed towards a man moving the chicken cages into the center of the ring.

Buckshot was wearing blue jeans with the cuffs turned up and a wool shirt and I knew that he had a wad of one-and two-dollar bills stuffed in his jeans pocket. He was incredible with money, and always managed to get a good deal.

Suddenly, a new current of excitement moved throughout the bleachers as Tommy Boyles', the owner of the auction pointed to a beautiful, full-plumed Rhode Island rooster that started clucking and strutting in the small wooden cage being carried into the auction pen. Tommy motioned for his helper to let the rooster out of his confinement. The auction pen was completely fenced off, and sensing his freedom, the magnificent fowl high-stepped around the arena with his head jutting forward and bobbing up and down with each jerking motion of his body.

Immediately realizing that he was the center of attention, the handsome cock stretched his proud head high, and with his neck feathers fluffed out and blowing gently in the light breeze, he let go a majestic "cock-a-doodle-doo." A murmur from the crowd raised the hopes of the waiting auctioneer, and Buckshot, now more determined than ever to own the rooster, pushed his way closer to the ring. Having seen Buckshot work the crowd at the auction before, I knew that he would go to any lengths to get the rooster home—and for the right price. "Hear the bid of five . . . now five and quarter . . . now five and a half," quickly intoned the eager and proficient auctioneer as people continued murmuring through the crowd. I saw Buckshot's eyes dilate, and his breathing became shallow as he stealthily crept towards the fence overlooking the coveted prize.

"Four dollars and fifty cents," he softly spoke into the vigilant crowd while the auctioneer recognized him learning over the fence. Smiling in his general direction, the auctioneer acknowledged that Buckshot was good for the bid. "We have a bid of four and half—now hear the bid for five," called out the auctioneer. For the next few minutes, people were nodding, using hand gestures and calling out bids as the tempo picked up for the right to own the magnificent rooster.

"Six twenty-five," spoke Buckshot to the loud and eager crowd. Within minutes, the bidding had reached eight dollars and twenty cents.

Not being discouraged and determined to own the magnificent breeding stock, Buckshot looked directly at the auctioneer, and in clear and confident voice said, "Eight dollars and seventy-five cents."

Silence followed. Heads turned and looked all around the arena, and like music to both our ears, the auctioneer ended the misery by affirming: "8.75 once, 8.75 twice . . . sold."

Over the next hour, Buckshot bought four sturdy-looking hens, and after enjoying a donut and cherry Coke in the café, we headed back to his place with the clucking and agitated fowl in the back of his dad's truck.

Over the next few years, Buckshot and I continued to buy, sell, and trade jalopies and everything else that we thought would make us rich. My last vehicle before joining the Navy was a 1956 Ford Crown Victoria V8 flathead. It was the envy of the town, and I spent countless hours rebuilding and repainting the vehicle. Unfortunately, after spending nearly eight hundred dollars on a new paint job, one of my friends vomited out the window while riding home from "a party," and the new paint job became a thing of the past.

Six months after selling the Crown Victoria, and while doing basic training in Cornwallis, Nova Scotia, my Divisional Chief approached me and said that the Base Commander wanted to see me. I was terrified, as the scuttlebutt was that if you ever got that high up in trouble, you were guaranteed to get a nosebleed.

Standing before the four-ringed Navy Captain, it was revealed that my 1956 Ford had been involved in a motor vehicle accident; the driver had left the scene, and because I was still the registered owner, the local RCMP had a warrant for my arrest.

In short order, I was able to stammer and stutter to the brass that I had sold the vehicle before leaving town, and that my mother would be able to clear up the matter. What was painfully obvious was that "the friend" who had bought my car several days before I left for Halifax, Nova Scotia, had forgotten to buy insurance and register the vehicle in his name as promised. My mistake had been not making sure that the vehicle had been transferred to the new owner before leaving town; a valuable lesson to learn at the age of eighteen.

Chapter 6
The Logging Years

There came a time when Buckshot and I briefly went separate ways. I had joined the Navy, and Buckshot was operating his logging company. However, there was never a time when we did not know where the other one was. It was very comforting, as we were pals for life, and no matter what time of the day or night it was, we needed only to call each other for help. Buckshot once said to me, "Johnnycakes, if you get into trouble, let me know and I'll be there." Sure enough, if I got stuck on the mountain or the Malahat pass in a snowstorm in the middle of the night, I merely needed to phone Buckshot, and even if he had to leave for his logging camp in the morning, he would get out of his warm bed and come to my aid. He was extremely loyal, and we could always count on each other to be available for any emergency.

After Basic Training in Cornwallis, Nova Scotia, I was temporarily attached to HMCS Stadacona, the Navy barracks in Halifax. While waiting for a trades training course in Montreal, Quebec, I went to sea for six weeks on the Second World War frigate HMCS *New Waterford*. It was during a trip to the Azores that I made a decision to stay on the west coast as long as possible. The east coast sailors referred to us west coast lads as "sandy bottomers," as they thought that the South Pacific was a pond compared to the vast Atlantic.

After completing three months of trades training at HMCS Hochelaga, in Ville LaSalle, a suburb of Montreal, I was posted to the destroyer escort HMCS *St. Croix* in Esquimalt, BC.

When my warship was in home port at HMC Dockyard in Esquimalt, approximately fifty-five minutes south of my hometown of Duncan, I would spend some weekends in the Cowichan Valley, unless I was on duty. I could generally find Buckshot unless he was in his logging camp.

One particular time, in the summer of 1971, while serving on the submarine HMCS *Rainbow*, I received a call from Buckshot regarding a business chat.

By the time he was twenty, Buckshot had become a successful logger, and although he usually hired a small crew, he was extremely dedicated and made good money. I also knew that he demanded a full day's work for a full day's pay.

So, meeting up with him that particular afternoon in 1971, Buckshot took me for a ride in his company truck. As we neared a long stretch of highway, north of Mill Bay, Buckshot pulled over to the side of the road and told me that he had just bought the acreage on our right. I was not surprised as he was always buying, trading, and selling land. He would buy a chunk of land, selectively log it, and then sell the logs to the best market and either keep the land or sell the land so that he could start the process over again. Looking at the lush and densely treed property, I asked him what his plans were this time.

"Johnnycakes, it's time for you to get out of the Navy and become my business partner," was his excited answer to my fearful question.

Looking directly at Buckshot, I was visibly shaken by his comment, as I had just finished my first five-year tour and had recently signed an Indefinite Engagement Contract for thirty years' military service—which meant I had to serve a minimum of twenty-four more years in the Navy.

"Why?" was my monosyllabic response. His rather long and uncharacteristic response to my cryptic reply came as a further surprise:

"We're going to clear the property and build a neighborhood pub, and I would like you to manage it so that I can continue operating my logging company. Johnnycakes, I trust you, and I know that you will make a good business manager."

I sensed from watching the business market and the incumbent government's supportive small business policies and, the fact that there were very few Neighborhood pubs on Vancouver Island that a pub on this spot would certainly be financially lucrative. "I have three weeks shore leave coming, so why don't we begin logging and clearing now?" I suggested.

Buckshot smiled and responded, "I'll start falling trees next week, and you can show up when you get your leave approved." What was interesting was that his brother had been in the Navy for the past twelve years, so his knowledge of military administration saved me considerable explanation.

***

The following week, Buckshot moved his logging equipment onto the five-acre parcel, and the two of us logged and cleared an area where we wanted to build our pub and a wine and beer store. The work was grueling, and the first three days nearly did me in; I had spent the last three years at sea, and although my sea legs were in good shape, my back continually protested.

The first morning on the job, Buckshot took me on a tour of the acreage. It was evident that he had been felling trees the weekend before I started, as the entire lot was a mess of logs, boughs, and slash. Struggling through the waist-high felled trees, I groaned in anticipation of my first logging job.

The boughs were as thick as my forearms where they had been joined to the tree, and the severed branches stuck out at every angle. It was a nightmare just walking through the fallen trees. Waving his hands around in a 360-degree arc, Buckshot said, "Okay, sailor, your job is to separate the branches away from the trees, hook up the chokers, set the eye of the sling on my skidder, and raise your arm in the air so I can drag them to the landing. "

Being ill-informed about being on a logging site, I asked the sorriest question of my miserable life: "What and where are the choker cables?"

With a frown on his weather-beaten face, Buckshot pointed to the back of his skidder.

Staggering through the pile of snarled boughs and "helter-skelter" forest of five-foot-around fir trees, I managed to reach the back of his log skidder after tangling up in the boughs and falling down a few times.

I was exhausted just getting to the back of the skidder, and I felt an ominous dread course through my body. I was bruised, battered, discouraged, and had not yet started work. The machine was not very big, but definitely adequate for the task at hand, although Buckshot owned much larger skidders in his logging company.

The machine looked to be about eight feet high, and it had huge rubber tires with treads about six inches apart. The front of the skidder had a moveable blade that was half raised at the time. Behind the driver's seat, and at the very back of the winch gear, there was tangle of wire cables about fifteen to twenty feet long. Buckshot explained that the cables were in fact chokers, and that there were longer ones over on a pile by the tree line.

Glancing over at the tree line, about two hundred feet west of my position, I quickly realized that it would take an act of God for me to thrash my way over in that direction. My fervent prayer was that I would not need the heavier cables.

Jumping up in the seat of the skidder, Buckshot pushed the starter and a black cloud of rancid diesel smoke blasted in my face. Buckshot, an experienced logger of about ten years, waved his arms over at the pile of tangled trees and yelled for me to follow behind the skidder. I immediately thought of my brief time serving with the army, where I had been required to follow along behind a tank.

Watching to make sure that Buckshot was not going to mow me down with the skidder, I staggered through the slash and waited for him to back up to a large tree lying in the heap. The skidder could easily ride up over branches and trees, and to my discouragement, the machine was breaking and crushing some of the tangled boughs—which meant more work for me later.

When the skidder was about fifteen feet from the tree, Buckshot motioned for me to grab a cable off the back of the skidder and connect it to the designated log. Trudging once again through the slash, I grabbed a cable and nearly ripped my hand open on the spines of the partially frayed cable.

Jumping back and thinking that I had a worker's compensation claim within the first three minutes of being on the job, Buckshot, seeing me jumping around with blood dripping from my soft and tender hands, shut off the machine and jumped down to the ground.

For the first time, Buckshot seemed to notice that I was dressed in my Navy dungarees and leather sea boots, which offered absolutely no protection from the hazards of logging equipment. "Where are your safety boots and gloves?" he intoned.

Grasping my torn hand, I lamented that no one had told me that I needed safety equipment. Grinning, Buckshot waved me over to his pickup truck and told me to get what I needed out of the cab. Several minutes later, I came back rigged with cork boots and faller's pants and gloves. Unfortunately, we were on the time clock, and I did not have time to bandage my bleeding hand, although I did manage to wrap a piece of tissue paper over the slightly scraped and still bleeding wound.

"Okay, Johnnycakes, we lost half the morning now, and we haven't dragged a single log to the landing. Let's get rippin'. Are you ready?"

My feeble nod was enough to get him back on the skidder. Looking down at me from his comfortable perch, Buckshot backed up a few more feet and indicated that I was to hook up the choker cable. Carefully, I took the choker off the back of the skidder, dragged it over to the three-foot round fir, and came to my second dilemma of the morning. Not knowing how to hook the choker to the log, I look over at Buckshot with a question on my face.

With the skidder chugging away, Buckshot started waving his arms around in an effort to mime how I should hook the cable to the rough and "knotty" tree lying amidst the nasty looking and twisted boughs. Finally, I started thinking like a sailor working the upper deck of a ship and thought about the lines and cables that we used to raise and lower items on the upper deck. Bending over, I hooked the cable around the end of the log and ran it back to the skidder, hooked the eye over the shackle end, and jumped back with a smug look on my face.

Buckshot appeared to be surprised at my new-found dexterity, and a smile of hope flitted across his face. Jumping out of the way, Buckshot manipulated the levers, and to my evident pride, the gnarly fir tree began to side and slither over the pile of trees on the ground and ran a course toward the skidder. With a whoop, Buckshot started moving forward, dragging the first log of the morning.

Before I could gloat that I had reached the competent level of a choker man, the cable slid off the log and the skidder shot forward as there was no longer a load on the cable.

Slamming to a halt, Buckshot jumped down from the idling skidder, strode over to the separated choker, glanced quickly in my direction, and waved a huge meaty hand in my face. Ready to turn in my logging gear, I gingerly made my way back to the waiting log. "Johnnycakes, what do you guys learn in the Navy? Surely you must know how to hook a cable to something onboard a ship?"

"Show me," was all I managed to mumble.

Buckshot leaned over the log, grabbed the choker, and wrapped the noose of the cable under and around the tree, brought the noose back into the eye, tugged on the noose, and then handed me the cable end with the following instructions: "Now, that there is tension on the choker. The strain from the winch will tighten on the cable eye, and the choker will tighten on the end of the log. Presto—we move one over to the landing."

Well, sure enough, we managed to drag the first log over to the landing at around 11:55 a.m., at which point I signaled for a break. Unfortunately, Buckshot was on a roll, and five hours later we stopped for something to eat.

By the end of the day, I was incapable of complaining, as all my energy was gone and my feet felt like there was lead in my boots. As we were leaving just before dark, four hours after the snack, Buckshot quietly said, "See you bright and early, as we have a ten-hour day tomorrow."

Sure enough, within the three weeks, we had logged, cleared, and leveled the site. Buckshot looked at his work with pride and suggested that I start the paperwork for a licence and building permit. There were still lots of things to be done; however, Buckshot told me to go back to the

Navy, put in for a release, and that he would finish cleaning up the site.

***

When my twenty-one-day shore leave was over, I seriously began to think about the political climate vis-à-vis building a neighborhood pub. The positive thing was that some of my shipmates noticed that I had lost about ten pounds. I had always been fairly muscular from working in the saw mills, running marathons, and boxing. However, the past three years at sea had taken a toll on my physical strength; in addition to injuring my cervical spine while at anchor onboard the warship HMCS *Columbia*.

At that particular time, in the fall of 1971, a political wind was wafting through the incumbent government, and I had a concern that if I put in a release from the Navy and the government changed, I could very well be unemployed. Several weeks later, Buckshot asked me how things were going, and I advised him that I had started the legal work and that we needed a public referendum for the liquor licence. I also shared that rumors were flying around that the Opposition Party were eager for an election call, and that the leader of the Opposition Party was fairly confident that their party could form a government when the election call came.

It was a sobering thought, as we did not want to have to start over again with a new government; however, we continued forward and tentatively lined up all our ducks in a row for an impending Neighborhood pub.

Nearly ready to begin development, the incumbent Social Credit Government, who had been in power in British Columbia since 1952, "dropped the writ," and to the surprise of most British Columbians, including Buckshot and I, the Opposition won the election and formed a majority government. It was devastating, and it immediately put our project on hold.

Conversely, I was greatly relieved that I had not tendered my release from the Navy. Within six months of the new government taking power, we knew that a Neighborhood pub licence was out of reach. To our relief, the new government only remained in power for three years and was defeated by the Social Credit government in the next general election of 1975.

For the next eighteen years, I continued with my Navy career and served with land forces and sailed all over the world while maintaining a close contact with Buckshot. We still managed to go hunting and fishing and socialize whenever the time became available. Our friendship was solid, and time and distance had little effect on our commitment as friends. The most difficult time in my military career was my first posting to the Middle

East. I saw service in Egypt, Israel, Syria, and Lebanon. I was attached to the Austrian Battalion, while posted to the 73 Canadian Signal Troop, headquartered in Damascus, Syria, under the auspices of the United Nations Dis-engagement Observer Force.

The experience dramatically changed my life. I was exposed to horrendous atrocities in Syria, Lebanon and Egypt, and those experiences left an indelible scar on my psyche. I have written many short stories on the suffering in the Middle East and Eastern countries. The Jabalia Palestinian refugee camp in the Gaza Strip was one of those horrible experiences.

During my military service career, I traveled the globe, and thankfully there were more good times than not-so-good times. Our navy ships sailed the entire world, and I enjoyed encountering different cultures in many countries. In addition, my wife Gloria and I went on two world trips as self-supporting evangelical missionaries upon my retirement from military service.

During that time, Buckshot continued operating his logging company and spent most of his working days on the northern part of Vancouver Island, thereby being in a position to live on Turn Island. He was well respected by his crew and had always made payroll, thereby keeping his men working.

The fact that I was serving in the military gave me a special bond with my father, who had served in the Canadian Army during the Second World War. In addition, Buckshot shared a special relationship with my dad as a result of our friendship and scouting experiences.

Visiting my dad one day at his home in Duncan, he casually commented that every winter for the past six or seven years someone had been dumping dry split firewood on his carport. I shared with him that it might have been Buckshot, and I was surprised to see tears in my tough old dad's eyes as he asked me to invite Buckshot to the house for a visit. I remember as a child that my dad would invite not-so prosperous people to our home and empty our deep freezer of meat and bless those people with food from our cupboards. When asked about his generosity, he would explain that as a prisoner of war he was lucky to get a full meal and that being hungry was a painful thing to endure. I also recalled that he only ate small portions on his plate and refused to see food go to waste. He used to say; "I eat to live, not live to eat."

The following weekend, Buckshot and I spent the afternoon with my dad. What was most delightful about the visit was the fact that Buckshot had not seen my father in about fifteen years, and without preamble he called him "sir," which visibly affected my father.

When my father tried to pay Buckshot for the years of firewood, Buckshot flatly refused to discuss the matter. I know my dad was really affected by the generous gift of firewood, as my parents had a fireplace in the living room that rarely had been used due to the exorbitant cost of seasoned firewood. I was delighted that Buckshot had more than atoned for the gasoline that he siphoned from his Scoutmaster's car many years earlier.

On occasion, I would visit with Buckshot in his logging camps on Vancouver Island. This was also a treat, as his wife Cheryll and their two young daughters worked in the camp kitchen to the delight of the entire crew. The camp food was exceptional, and there was always plenty of excitement in learning about the logging operation.

Watching Buckshot fall a tree was an amazing thing to witness. He was a natural faller, and he had taught himself at an early age. It was apparent that he became "one with the tree" as he walked around checking the wind, measuring how big the undercut should be, and where he was going to fall the tree so that he could limb the branches and mark off the length he wanted before bucking it for the sawmill; he could also determine how much board feet of lumber the tree would eventually produce.

***

Several years later, while serving with the Communications Group (Western Group) HQ's in Jericho Beach, West Vancouver, and sitting under a large dining tent in the backyard on a Saturday afternoon, I saw a motorhome drive onto the military base. I had no idea who it was, and I went back to reading my book. Several minutes later, I heard joyful laughter beside the tent, and looking up I saw Buckshot, his wife, and two young daughters standing on the lawn. I whooped with joy and found out that they had just finished a two-week camping trip in the motorhome and were on their way back to Vancouver Island.

They stayed with us for two days, and our daughters Cindy, Dianna, Dawn, and son Les had a wonderful time with their daughters Brenda and Roxanne. It had been about three years since the girls had seen each other, as we had just gotten back from a posting in Ontario. I recall the day they arrived, as the news was full of the sudden passing of Elvis Presley.

Two years later in 1979, while attending Simon Fraser University as a mature student, I was sent to the Middle East on a United Nations Tour in Syria and the Golan Heights in Israel. Immediately after returning from overseas, I found the opportunity to see Buckshot, as I suspected that I was being posted out of province in the summer of 1980. During my next posting tour, I was employed as the Senior Administrator and Trades Training NCO at the Military Police School in Camp Borden, Ontario. As a reward for serving out of province again (for the third time in less than seventeen years), I was posted back to Vancouver Island in July 1983. It was wonderful being back on Vancouver Island, and Buckshot and I saw each other as often as we could and took every opportunity to go fishing and hunting. These were good times, and we shared many more adventures.

On July 7, 1983, I was posted to the warship HMCS *Yukon*, and in early September we set sail for South America and were at sea for three months. During the ship's nine month refit in 1984, I commenced studies at the University of Victoria. After refit our ship continued Operations with the Second Destroyer Squadron based out of Esquimalt.

***

In the summer of 1986, Buckshot was logging in the Campbell River area and got word to me though my father that he would be coming out of the bush and would like to meet me in Campbell River. Getting the good news, I made a decision to take some well-earned shore leave and made arrangements to meet him up Island.

It was a well-known fact on Vancouver Island that loggers worked hard, and, conversely, played hard.

With that thought in mind, one can imagine a crew of bushed loggers hitting town with the only thought of spending their payroll at the nearest bar. I remember getting a ride to Campbell River with a former employee of Buckshot's who was going to see him about a job.

Later that afternoon, we met up with my buddy Buckshot who I had not seen for about eight months. The first order of business was Buckshot getting the contract log broker to pay him off for the timber he had recently taken out of the woods.

It was a significant amount of money owing to his company, and there was a delay in the payment. Knowing Buckshot as I did, it was becoming evident that he was beginning to worry about paying off his crew; but as was his custom, rich or poor, Buckshot always kept his word and took care of his crew.

Meeting him at the Quinsum Hotel, a rough-and-tumble establishment in the Campbell River area, Buckshot had to put his crew up in the hotel and cover all their living expenses and slake their thirst until the broker paid him for the timber. For two days, I watched Buckshot taking care of his thirsty crew of nearly penniless loggers. Wearing cork boots, ripped and torn faller pants held up by wide suspenders, and gray Stanfield thermal work sweaters covered with sawdust, dirt, and ten days of grime, the loggers imbibed in the bar. They were a dirty but happy crew. Most of the locals knew that Buckshot always carried a pocket full of fifty- and hundred-dollar bills when his crew came out of the woods, and they looked forward to his patronage.

On this occasion, Buckshot was waiting for his money and had to resort to spending personal funds that he desperately needed for payroll. Being the honorable employer that he was, Buckshot moved from table to table where his crew was eating, drinking, and partying in antici- pation of a payday, and after sitting with them for a few minutes, he would drop a fifty-dollar bill on the table and move on to the next group.

He did this for two days without a murmur of complaint. Several days later, he shared with me in confidence that he was concerned that he was not going to be able to pay off his crew, as the log broker had still not paid him for the timber. Dejected but the ever-stalwart employer, he drove down island with the dregs of his bedraggled crew in the back of his one-ton pickup truck.

The first pullover was Courtenay, where we stopped at a place for a drink and something to eat. I had been trying to get Buckshot's attention all morning, as I was in the box of the truck while we were going south. Finally, during lunch, I was able to learn that he needed about two thousand dollars so that he could make a bank deposit and write paychecks for his small crew.

Sitting at a table, I looked directly at Buckshot and said in a hushed voice so that no one else could hear, "Do you remember going from table to table, dropping big bills all day long for two days in the Quinsum Hotel?"

With a twisted and pained look on his face, he groaned and said, "Yeah, how I wish I had that money now."

Hearing those words, I reached into my pocket and pulled out a huge wad of money.

"What's that you have in your hand?" he asked with eager anticipation.

I replied, "I followed behind you and scooped up the change every time you bought the first round."

The smile on his face warmed my heart, and with the light back in his eyes, I handed him nearly $1,800 plus a handful of coins. Altogether, he had spent about $2,000 looking after his crew, and the $1,800 would take a huge bite out of the payroll commitment.

The Logging Years

***

One day several months after our trip out of Campbell River, I came across Buckshot in Duncan. After catching up on personal news, we headed back to his A-frame house on Fischer Road. I had been away at sea when he built the house and was amazed at the design of the home. Taking a tour through the unique construction was breathtaking, as he had built the house with material purchased over the years at garage sales and items from his parent's antique store. The staircase from the main floor to the upper rooms was offset from the huge open kitchen and dining room and was made from black wrought iron.

The staircase spiraled upwards in a nearly vertical position, and the windows in both the kitchen and bathrooms were made of antique leaded and colored glass. The bedroom doors were pre-Victorian heritage and the upper part of the door was encased with cathedral art and colored leaded glass.

Upon exiting the house, I noticed that the backyard was completely covered in old-growth trees, and behind a fenced area he had parked his logging equipment: trucks, fuel bowsers, skidders, and all types of gas and diesel containers. In the side driveway, there were four or five crew cab pickup trucks, and he explained that his son-in-law was living on the property and that his daughter Brenda had been cooking in his logging camp.

While walking in the forest behind the equipment, I noticed a little black cocker spaniel trotting nimbly several feet behind us, and I made an innocuous comment regarding the dog: "How old is Poncho now? You seem to have had him for quite a long time."

He replied, in that deadpan manner he was known for, "Which one do you mean? I've had about five black cocker spaniels, all named Poncho." He was indeed a mysterious guy.

Buckshot was a man of many different talents, and he could operate any type of equipment and machinery, whether the machine was a Bobcat, excavator, or fully loaded logging truck.

His strength and energy were legendary; whether he was falling trees, clearing land, digging holes, pushing earth, or just messing around on log skidders, he was always up to the task. In fact, as soon as he jumped into the cab of a particular piece of machinery, it only took a few minutes before he was able to work the controls, even though he had never been in the machine before.

It was amazing that Buckshot had spent his entire working life in the forest and had never been injured. However, he eventually shared a story about one of the worst days of his logging life. He remonstrated that he had been driving a fully loaded logging truck down a steep and dusty logging road in late August, and coming to a hairpin turn in the road, the air brakes failed. I had never heard my friend speak with such intensity as he told me the story of seeing his life flash before his eyes as the truck, loaded to the top of the bunkers with green timber, pushed the already speeding truck down the switch-back mountain road.

The faster he went, the more he tried to ditch the truck. Thinking that his wife and daughters would never see him again, he jerked the steering wheel hard to the right and slipped sideways against the dirt bank and skidded downhill for several hundred feet, dragging dirt, rocks, and small trees, finally coming to rest several hundred yards short of a two-hundred-foot drop.

He said he looked all around the cab of the truck, checked his arms and legs for broken bones, and slowly crawled from the bent and broken cab. Shaking on the side of the road, he recalled rolling a cigarette and thinking that the angels had been with him on that particular day.

It was a chilling story, and I thanked God that he had survived the ordeal, as the newspapers were full of logging fatalities.

It was amazing the Buckshot had been a faller for over twenty-five years and had never been seriously injured in the woods.

***

On December 31, 1988, I officially retired from the military as a Lieutenant and transferred to the Supplementary Reserves. Prior to moving back to the beautiful Cowichan Valley, I was offered a position as a Corrections Officer at the Vancouver Island Regional Correctional Centre. After working in the institution for about eleven months, I was successful in obtaining a position with the Provincial Emergency Program as the Northern Region Zone Manager. It was an entirely new zone, and my job was to organize fifteen communities in the area of Disaster Management within the Prince Rupert RCMP Subdivision.

My area of responsibility covered over two hundred thousand square miles, stretching from the Yukon border south to Kitimat, BC, and east from Bella Coola and west to Huston, BC. It was an amazing job, as my mandate was to "mitigate human suffering and save lives." As a Peace Officer, I thoroughly enjoyed the challenges. The following year, I was seconded into the Parliament buildings in Victoria and served as an Executive Assistant and, later, a Ministerial Assistant to two Provincial Cabinet Ministers.

Finally, after serving more than twenty-seven years in the Federal and Provincial Governments, I left government work in the summer of 1990 and started a Private Investigations Company, which became a lucrative source of income for many years. My trade name was "Ace," and that moniker served me well for the next twenty-eight years.

In the fall of 1991, the Social Credit Government was defeated by the New Democrats, and once again major changes affected the logging industry. It was the second time since 1972 that the Social Credit Government had been defeated by the New Democrat Party.

At about the same time that the new government came into power, Buckshot's father, Wilf, became suddenly ill and passed away in November 1991. Buckshot was devastated, and he shut down his logging company so that his family could deal with Wilf's passing.

Buckshot and his father had been very close, and the sudden passing of his seventy-three-year-old father had a profound effect on him. I was deeply humbled to be there during his time of grief and had the honor of officiating his father's Celebration of Life.

Several months after his father passed away, Buckshot decided that he was ready to go back to work in his logging company. Unfortunately, during this time of grieving, the new government exponentially increased timber stumpage fees, and for the first time in twenty-seven years of logging, Buckshot was out of work.

Not to be daunted, Buckshot rallied and started working as an equipment operator for a concrete company in the Valley. In addition, he started a firewood operation and spent the rest of his life falling, cutting, and selling firewood. At times there were logging truck piles of bucked timber stacked eight feet high in his backyard, and the sound of his power saw and wood splitter were common to the neighborhood.

As Buckshot settled into semi-retirement, garage sales abounded and both he and his wife spent most of their spare time buying and selling at various local buy, sell, and trade marts. It was fun to meet them at the selling marts, and to my chagrin, my wife got the garage sale fever, which further distanced me from junk dealing. However, thanks to Buckshot, Gloria found some rare antiques.

Most mornings, Buckshot would take off in his white pickup truck with gas cans, a power saw, and his dog Sheila as they headed out to some remote place in the bush to fill the truck with firewood. It was interesting to see him coming back with wood rounds piled high above the truck cab, and the power saw nestled in the wood at the top.

If he was not cutting wood, fishing, or going to garage sales, he was traveling. There was no grass growing under his feet, as he was always doing something. Buckshot was an inspiration, and I enjoyed getting a phone call from him early in the morning, as it usually meant another adventure.

Chapter 7
A New Beginning

The next few years raced by in a blur, although Buckshot and I managed to continue our adventures. Fishing and hunting took on a new meaning, and many weekends and summers were spent fishing off Buckshot's island and out of the San Juan River in Port Renfrew. In addition to the boating jaunts, Buckshot, me, and our wives took trips across the USA border in our Westphalia van and spent wonderful times at garage sales and playing the slots for fun in the casinos.

On one particular occasion, my wife, my mother and I decided to pack our overnight gear and head across the United States border for some entertainment. Not being able to reach Buckshot at his home (he flatly refused to own a telephone answering machine), we headed out of town. As we crossed the border at Blaine, Washington, and headed about forty-five miles south on the I-5 Highway, it began to rain, and I quickly decided to pull off into a motel that we had found the year before. I drove into the parking space in front of the motel, and in complete darkness, I began exiting my vehicle. As I was getting out of our truck, I noticed a light gray station wagon parked on the passenger side of my vehicle. Thinking the vehicle looked like Buckshot's van, but ignoring my intuition as we were in a foreign country and the odds were beyond computation, I walked into the lobby of the motel. Waiting to check in, I turned to look out the window of the lobby and thought I saw a rather husky male who looked very much like Buckshot sleeping in the back seat of the van. His head was back against the headrest, and his eyes were closed. Well, shiver my nautical timbers; it had to be Buckshot, as no one I had ever known reposed like him. Turning to go back outside, Buckshot's wife called out my name from the front counter. Well, we just roared with laughter, because both Buckshot and I had brought our wives and mothers on a trip to the states. It was incredibly funny, as my mother and his mother had known each other for a long time. Our coincidental meeting marked a new beginning of traveling together, and for the next three days, the six of us had a grand time full of card games, laughter, eating at good restaurants, and spending a bit of money at the local casinos.

My buddy Buckshot had many other talents, and playing poker was one of them. He had been raised on cards, and he could play every poker game known to mankind—and win he did, usually at my expense, because no matter how hard I tried, I always paid him out. Conversely, Buckshot was the most unlucky slot machine gambler in the west. He would stride into the casino and head straight for the greediest machine in the place. I tried to tell him many times that he had to walk around, watch the machine for a few minutes, and only spin the wheel a few times unless he won something.

Within fifteen minutes of entering the place, he would come over to my machine with a long, sad face, and through his teeth he'd say, "Johnnycakes, this place is a rip-off. I spent everything I brought with me, and left the rest at the motel, now "gettim" an expression that meant to get "them" meaning the casino. Knowing that he was always good on his word, I reached into my pocket and peeled off a large denomination bill. Off he would go, only to come back for more.

On this particular trip, the women decided to go shopping and Buckshot and I went two miles up the highway to the Angel of the Winds Casino. Well, Buckshot knew that I was really lucky with slot machines no matter where I went in the world. Anyhow, on this night in particular, I told Buckshot that he should sit beside me and save his money. Well, sure enough, he sat down beside me, and as luck would have it, I won nearly every spin on the machine. Growing impatient, Buckshot told me that he was ready to go out on his own. As he was walking away with good expectations of winning, I said during a winning spin, "Hey, Buckshot, watch the combinations, and don't stay too long on one machine." I got no reply as he lumbered away.

About an hour later, while walking around the casino looking for Buckshot, I found him at a penny machine in an absolute state of elation. Sitting beside him, I asked the 64,000-dollar question: "How are you making out?"

He turned to me with a big grin on his face and proudly boasted that he was up about seven hundred pennies. I doubled over with laughter and finally realized that it was not the amount of money he won, it was the fact that he won at all. I told him to stick with the pennies while I was going to cash out my $850 ticket.

We had many wonderful trips together, and I get a smile on my face every time I think of Buckshot winning a bunch of pennies; it was kind of neat for a guy who had made a substantial income from clear-cutting the forests.

After acquiring a rather secure base of clients in my investigations company, I decided to open an office in a trailer park in Victoria, as we had recently built a new ocean-view home on Balsam Avenue at Cherry Point Beach. The drive from Cobble Hill to Victoria, where the majority of my clients and work was located, became quite time-consuming with the daily commute. As chance would have it, an acquaintance from the shipyards told me that he was selling a deregistered mobile home in a well-established mobile home park. Jumping at the deal, we bought the unit and set about renovating; however, the job was far more demanding than my busy work schedule allowed, so I hired Buckshot to help my wife Gloria renovate the unit. When I had started our small business three years earlier, I did not expect success as quickly as it happened. In 1993, my wife Gloria resigned from her position as a Community Development Worker with the Native Friendship Centre and started working as an Apprentice Investigator in our company.

The majority of our work was in the civil litigation field, and more and more law firms and insurance companies were making demands for our services. In addition, I was becoming well known in the criminal defence area of investigations and the Department of Justice began hiring me in the defense of police officers. I investigated hundreds of criminal files: homicides, police shootings, armed robberies, fraud files, and sexual assault cases.

Working long and stressful hours every day while training Gloria in the art of surveillance, we continued to expand our lucrative and exciting business.

One morning, in the mid-1990s I phoned Buckshot at home and asked if he would like to come with me to Victoria, as I had an appointment and needed a day off from the busy investigation work. He agreed, I picked him up at his home, and we headed off to the capital city.

We arrived near the building where I had my appointment. While parking my private vehicle (the one with the non-tinted windows), I noticed the subject of one of my investigations parking his vehicle in front of mine.

The claimant had been quite elusive the past few weeks and I wanted to find out what he was doing. Quickly, I told Buckshot that I wanted him to watch the claimant, take notes, and find out where he was going—all without being seen. He excitedly agreed, and I excited the vehicle and went to my appointment.

Returning to the vehicle about forty-five minutes later, I noticed that the claimant's vehicle was gone. Walking around my vehicle, and trying to determine if the target was anywhere nearby, I noticed Buckshot flopped back in the front seat of my car with his head lolled over against the window, snoring in the bright sunlight. His mouth was agape, and people on the street walking by the car were chuckling at the sight of the contented middle-aged male oblivious to his surroundings. Sighing with exasperation, I got into the car and drove away. I was amazed that he did not wake up until we were nearly home. His excuse for losing the claimant was that he had been watching videos all night at home and had not gotten much sleep. When I think back on it, this was indeed a hilarious moment.

***

Shortly after purchasing the manufactured home in Victoria, Buckshot and my wife began renovating the 52-by-17-foot deregistered mobile home. The building was on cinder blocks and fully dry walled, but it required some new exterior doors, major electrical work, window upgrades, and carpeting, and paint—renovation tasks that both Buckshot and Gloria were very good at doing. For the next eight weeks, they turned the place into a presentable office and a place where we could spend the night without driving over the Malahat after working a long and full day.

One day, Buckshot was outside refitting the windows when he noticed someone crouched down behind some bushes, watching the renovations of our office. Letting me know about the strange behavior, I immediately recognized the man as one of the owners of the mobile home park. Speaking with the individual revealed that the well-established park was in the process of rezoning the property and sending out eviction notices. It was very disturbing news, as we had not yet completed the renovations. However, we soon learned that we had one year to vacate.

Dismayed at this sudden change of plans because Residential (R3) zoning was mandated for mobile homes, and rare to find on Vancouver Island, Buckshot set about finding us a piece of R3 land to relocate the office within the next year. To our benefit, Buckshot had many relatives in the Cowichan Valley, and his grandfather had owned large acreages all over Cobble Hill.

About six months later, the three of us found a two-acre piece of land for sale off the Trans-Canada Highway, not far from where we were going to build our pub in 1972. It was perfect, and Buckshot "timber cruised" the property; making a point that there was significant value in the treed lot. Making an offer, we secured the property, and once again Buckshot was back logging. He was an exceptional faller, and watching him walk around a 75-to-100-foot old-growth cedar or fir tree was awesome to watch, as Buckshot literally talked to the trees. He would walk completely around the base of the tree, lovingly place his hands on the bark, and tilt his head to look high up into the boughs cascading out from the crown.

One particularly old-growth cedar tree towered over our proposed building site, and everyone but Buckshot thought it would be impossible to fall the monstrosity without destroying half the neighborhood.

On the arranged day, Buckshot arrived early in the morning resplendent in his work clothes. Parking his one-ton work truck off to the side, he pulled the biggest power saw that I have ever seen out of the bed of the vehicle. The saw must have weighed seventy-five pounds, with the blade at least six feet long; I could barely pick it up. After walking around the majestic, two-hundred-year-old cedar tree, Buckshot cocked his ear to the wind and readied the tree for falling. Everyone watching cleared off to a safe distance.

Watching him prepare the equipment, I asked, "Where do you plan on laying the tree?"

His response, as usual, was, "Where do you want it?"

I knew he was serious, as he could fall a tree in the middle of a crowded city and lay the tree exactly where he wanted.

He was truly one of the most proficient fallers I had ever seen. To think that he learned to fall trees at the age of sixteen is beyond comprehension; most professional fallers work in the woods for years before they are sufficiently trained to fall trees.

With eager anticipation, we watched him put on his earmuffs; the time was near. Those of us watching were like children waiting for something really exciting to happen. The anticipation was incredible, and my heart began to beat faster as I saw Buckshot take one last look around the tree, test the wind direction, and get ready to start the saw. Grasping the six-foot-long power saw in his right hand, Buckshot hefted it about three feet above the ground, grasped the pull cord in his left hand, and dropped the saw towards the ground. As the huge saw dropped, he yanked the starting cord with his left hand. It was done so quickly that it was hard to see that he had jerked the saw downwards while yanking the starter card. Instantly, the saw roared to life. With a look of pure joy on his face, he carefully walked to the base of the mammoth tree and started the undercut.

The tree base was nearly the same width as the length of the saw blade, and Buckshot continued the undercut while slowly moving around the tree. About ten minutes later, he pulled the saw out of the cut, and with one last look at the top of the tree, he started the overcut above the lower cut in the front of the tree. After finishing the overcut, he moved around to the other side of the tree, took another look up, over, and around, and then began the back cut. Slowly, inch by inch, he cut into the tree, stopping several times with the saw idling as he walked around to the front cut. Years earlier, Buckshot had told me that he could control the direction of the fall by wedging the tree around while sawing into the other side. In this case, his undercut was directly in line with the place he wanted to lay the tree.

If he had wanted to turn the tree and fall it in another direction, he could manipulate the tree by wedging it around. We got a nod from Buckshot, so we moved further back.

Several minutes later, he stopped, looked again at where he was going to lay the tree, and yelled those exciting words everyone likes to hear: "Timbeeeeeeeeeeeeeeer!" That majestic old-growth cedar, which had been towering above and proudly watching over the smaller trees in the forest, slowly began to lean forward, and with a deep groan and a slight shudder, crashed to the earth exactly where it was supposed to land.

***

Over the next three days, Buckshot felled seven fir trees, and for the first time in years, sunlight shone through what was left of the forest on our acreage. After removing the limbs and bucking each tree, and tossing the boughs onto a roaring fire, we readied the area for milling. A few days later, Buckshot and a friend of his brought a portable Wood-Mizer saw onto the property, and over the next three weeks they cut over thirty thousand board feet of cedar and fir.

For many years to come, we used the lumber to build a house, two large cedar decks, a shop, and several garden sheds. Nature had to be careful with Buckshot, as he took "no prisoners" in a forest of future logs.

Once the area for the house site was cleared, Buckshot brought his skidder in and cleared and leveled a place to set our company office on a cinder block foundation.

At the same time we were developing the two acres in Cobble Hill, my wife and I bought a 2.3-acre piece of bare land in Honeymoon Bay near Gordon Bay Park: the same place where I had spent the first nine years of my life. The property was flat, with two large groves of cedar and fir trees. The rest of the property was covered in small alder trees. The property was the on the corner of the old Cowichan Copper Mine Road (now Walton Road) and not far from the lake. It was meant to be our retirement property as we had sold our home at Cherry Point beach and a house in Victoria, and were presently living in our office at Cobble Hill.

Wanting to start building our home on the acreage, I implored Buckshot for his help. He told me that he needed a new skidder as the old one had worn out, and that he could buy a used one from a fellow on Salt Spring Island. I made a deal with him that I would buy the skidder if he would help us clear the land. He was elated, and we started right away. After pushing the small alders out of the way and bucking them up for firewood, we exposed a beautiful building lot with a southern exposure. We moved our twenty-five-foot travel trailer onto the lot, and the three of us got to work. Buckshot was happy to be working again, as he greatly missed his logging company. Within six weeks, we had cleared and selectively logged the acreage.

After selecting the building spot for the house, we located an old bunkhouse amongst the alder trees, and checking it out, we suspected that the building had been placed onto the land when the Nitinat Logging Camp, or Camp 3 as referred to in the former logging days (circa 1920s) had been dismantled in 1985. The Nitinat Lake Region derives its name from the Nitinaht (or Ditidaht) First Nations people that controlled an area from near Jordan River to Pachena Point, extending inland along Nitinat Lake and some of the adjacent valleys to as far East as Cowichan Lake. The former bunkhouse was full of window frames and what looked to be the remnants of the Nitinat local drinking establishment.

The old shiplap building was crammed to the rafters with metal urinals and framed glass windows, and we made a decision to burn it down rather than spend days hauling every-thing out.

As a professional fire investigator, I had no difficulty making arrangements with the local fire department to burn the monstrosity down. My wife, Buckshot, and I readied the building for burning. Clearing a wide area completely around the place, we doused the shop with diesel fuel, and I, the pyro man, struck the match. In a matter of minutes, the building was a roaring inferno. Black smoke billowed into the air, and down she went.

Buckshot yelled to me over the crackling of the fire, "Stand back, I'm going to move the skidder in closer and push some of the debris back onto the fire."

Minutes later, the building was gone, and the only part burning was the floor. Taking a closer look, we noticed for the first time that the building had been sitting on twelve-inch-thick creosoted bridge decking. This was annoying, because if we had known this, I would have tried to save the dearly cherished material.

Hours later, the remains of the building were still smoldering while we waited in the grove. When it had cooled down considerably, we approached the fire and noticed that the bridge beams had been placed over a large pit in the ground. The soil at that part of the property was like pea gravel and looking down into the hole we saw an antique Triumph sports car. The car was dismantled, and it had been hidden in the hole under the shed. Buckshot—the only real antique car dealer in the group—nearly cried when he saw the destroyed vehicle. The heat from the creosote floor beams had completely melted the engine block, body, and fenders of the sports car. We still think of that car to this very day, and we never did find out who had hidden it in the hole. I remember the history of the property, because I had played there as a young child. Back in the late '40s, a Chinese businessman bought the forty acres and someone later subdivided the acreage into 2.3 acre lots. As the area was quite remote we thought that maybe someone had dragged the bunkhouse and old car onto the lot and never came back to claim the items.

Buckshot pushed a circular driveway into the property with his skidder, and then made another driveway that circled around the first grove of evergreen trees that were off to the side of the building lot.

It was breathtaking, especially in the snow. Buckshot thinned out the grove, and in about eight months, we had built the house, shop, boat and RV storage building. The cedar and fir that we had milled on the Cobble Hill property was used for the decks around the house and most of the outbuildings.

At that time, I was fifty-one years old, and I began feeling tired halfway through the day, which was unusual, although I had first noticed in 1997 that my energy was waning during an International Investigators Course in Boston, Massachusetts. Having been a former long distance runner for over twenty years, I generally walked everywhere possible, and when I booked my hotel in Boston, it was for the purpose of walking to and from the conference center.

On the first day of the course, and while walking the three miles into the city, I noticed that I was perspiring an inordinate amount and short of breath. This continued over the next two years, and my only thought was that I was just getting older.

One afternoon, on December 16, 1999, while playing four-handed canasta in our Victoria company office with Buckshot and Cheryll, I fainted on the way to the bathroom and was rushed to Victoria General Hospital. After a few days in the hospital, I was told that I required open-heart surgery, and that the date was booked for March 6, 2000. However, due to deteriorating health, I went into the operating room late in the evening of December 31, 1999. I later learned that I was the last open-heart patient of the century in the City of Victoria at the Royal Jubilee Hospital. Sadly, I have no recollection of the millennium change on New Year's Eve 1999.

While I was recovering in the hospital from aortic valve replacement, our rezoning application for the Cobble Hill property completed phase two and was now ready for government permits.

Not being able to dig the septic percolation holes for inspection, I appointed Buckshot as my representative. It was a particularly cold and wet January, and Buckshot made contact with the ministry responsible for permits.

In a meeting with the health inspector, Buckshot was told to dig five, four foot-deep holes in a fifty square foot area for a septic field permit. Well, Buckshot was not pleased with those instructions, as he knew from generations of family experience around our land that holes that big would undermine the soil and fill with water.

Unfortunately, the health inspector made an error in judgement and ordered the holes be dug as directed. In a rare moment, Buckshot became angry and told the man that he was an idiot. Anyhow, the holes were dug, and the health ministry complained that the holes were full of water and no longer usable for a septic field. Buckshot was right, and nothing else could be done at that time. While I was lying in hospital recovering, Buckshot sat by my bed and shared how he had insulted the government guy and messed up my building permit.

Gingerly, I turned my head, looked at Buckshot, and said, "Don't worry; we can deal with him when I get out of here. Thanks for being there for me."

He was vastly relieved, as it was the first time in over forty years that I had seen him so upset. The good thing was that we eventually obtained all the permits and later sold the property for a small but well deserved profit.

Chapter 8
A New Career

In the fall of 1990, we moved back to the Cowichan Valley and I opened a Private investigations Company which my wife aptly named Ace Investigations. For about three years I worked the company establishing a solid base of clients. My wife Gloria was still working for the Native Friendship Center in Duncan. The business grew and I worked all over Vancouver Island. It was exciting work and I was able to draw from years of experience working with the government. As my name and company achievements became known, I was offered several high profile cases that made history. In addition, I was hired to investigate two criminal cases involving First Nations communities. The first case led to the successful prosecution of the educators and administrators responsible for the abuse of children at the Port Alberni Residential School. The second case led to the solving of the 1908 murder of eight year-old Residential School student Johnny Sticks, a member of the Secwepemc (Shuswap) First Nations people located at Alkali Lake in the Cariboo Region of BC.

About six years after establishing our company, I began working as an investigator for a retired Supreme Court Judge who had gone back into private practice. In 1998, I applied for a Security Guard Licence and began hiring staff and taking on Security Contracts in the Cowichan Valley. At that time we changed our name to Ace Investigations & Security. During a lunch meeting in Victoria in 1999, with the retired judge who I was working for in Victoria, he asked me if I would be interested in opening an investigations office in Oahu, Hawaii. He loved to golf, and the only way he could afford to regularly golf on the Hawaiian Islands was to have a business venture he could write off. Being that I was a Certified International Investigator, I jumped at the opportunity and told him that I would take a trip to Honolulu, formalize the United States Private Detective Certification; a formality required to work in the Hawaiian Islands, obtain American Certification, and open a small storefront office in Oahu.

Excited with the new prospect of starting up a satellite office in Hawaii, I phoned Buckshot that evening and asked him if he would like to spend seven days with me in Hawaii. Off we went the following Monday, arriving in Honolulu in the late afternoon. Buckshot was like a kid in a candy store, as he had spent his entire working life in the woods and seldom was able to get away from his firewood business and week-end garage sales. After checking in at our hotel, sixteen blocks from the beach, we went out for dinner and crashed early in the small room with the uncomfortable twin beds.

The following morning, I told Buckshot that I had to attend with the American Security Licensing Branch and that while I was challenging the exam, he might want to spend the day on the beach.

At around 8:45 a.m., I left Buckshot at the beach. Getting my bearings, I noted that he was all alone on a sandy part of the beach about a hundred yards from the public change room. When I walked away, Buckshot was reposing on the sand in his blue and green Bermuda shorts.

Five hours later, having finished my paperwork and being certified as a Private Detective in the State of Hawaii, I sauntered back to the beach and panicked. The beach was absolutely crowded. There must have been over five hundred people sitting, standing, and running around on the sandy beach. Frantically, I began looking in every direction and yelling "Buckshot!" at the top of my voice to the amazement of hundreds of beachgoers. Finally, I found the public change room and zeroed in on where Buckshot should have been earlier that morning.

Fearing that he might have left when the beach became crowded and not knowing how to get back to the Budget Inn, I pushed my way through the throng. Eventually, I found the spot where I had last seen Buckshot, and noticed about fifteen or twenty stunningly beautiful young women in various types of bathing attire, sitting in a large circle chatting freely.

Edging closer, I managed to look in the middle of the circle, and to my absolute chagrin, saw Buckshot fast asleep in the middle of the group of women.

Lying on his back and oblivious of everything around him, I heard a deep, even snore coming out of his open mouth. I also noticed that he was bright red from sun exposure. Assessing the situation, I looked at the young ladies, wondering how they could have carried on an animated conversation with Buckshot snoring in the middle of their group. It was utterly amazing, and once again I called his name. Slowly, Buckshot who had always been a deep sleeper, opened his eyes, shook his head in confusion several times, and thinking that he had died and gone to heaven, slowly rotated his head all around the circle, looking at the casual manner in which the ladies were conversing over his supine body. Not believing his good fortune, he rolled over on his side and went back to sleep.

After calling his name several more times, he got to his feet and we left. On the way back to the hotel, Buckshot seemed to have acquired a meaningful bounce in his step. We laughed about the incident for years, as Buckshot's only memory of waking up was looking at an endless sea of colorful bikinis.

Spending the next six days investigating a mail drop, small office space, and a phone service, we headed back to Canada. Unfortunately, the office in the Hawaiian Islands did not materialize, as the Internal Revenue Service in conjunction with Revenue Canada required joint tax filing in both countries, which greatly irked the retired judge who refused to pay double income tax. My company absorbed the trip to Hawaii, and Buckshot and I did not speak about those expenses.

***

Over the next few years, Buckshot and I made a decision to spend more time boating, fishing, and hunting on his island. I had fully recovered from the aortic valve replacement operation and started back in my company with renewed vigor, and between 2001 and 2004, we had over twenty-one employees in our security business, which was serving us well. As hiring security guards was difficult due to the demand for trained personnel, I opened a Security Training School and taught Basic Security Courses under the name of Ace Security Academy so that I would have a ready list of certified guards on hand for our various security contracts.

On June 27, 2004, my father, Robert Vincent Waddy succumbed to a myocardial infarction and passed away with all the flags flying on Canada Day, July 1. It was devastating to our family, as he was only eighty-three years old. Being a former prisoner of war at the age of twenty-one had taken a toll on his quality of life. He was a wonderful and well-respected man with a great sense of humor and every Scout in the Cowichan Valley had loved him. There were over four hundred mourners crammed into the church, and many more on the street outside during his full military funeral. I had the honour of officiating my father's Celebration of Life; and Buckshot, my Brother Don, two former Scouts, a Victoria City Police Detective, and Ross, a long-time family friend, carried his coffin to the waiting hearse.

Several days before he passed away, he asked me to straighten out the history books regarding the misinformation recorded about the disastrous Dieppe Raid. Eleven months after he passed away, I made my first of three separate trips to Dieppe, France, and with the assistance of the Dieppe War Museum and the French Minister of National Defense, I cleared up the record regarding my father's artillery unit during the raid.

The error was that in 1941, while the Canadian Army Second Division Commandoes were training with Lord Lovat on the Isle of Wight, my father's unit, the Sixteenth Canadian Light Anti-Aircraft Unit, was ordered to amalgamate with the Third Canadian Anti-Aircraft Unit and join forces with the Royal Regiment of Canada. After the Royal Regiment of Canada was nearly annihilated at Puys Beach on that fateful day of August 19, 1942, the military records did not record the Sixteenth Canadian Light Anti-Aircraft Unit as having been on the Dieppe Raid.

It took me nearly three years to correct the errors, and when it was proven that the facts had been incorrect, I wrote a short story called "Dad's Dieppe," which was published in the *Legion Magazine* and the *Command Lookout Newspaper* at Canadian Forces Base Esquimalt. The last trip to Dieppe, France, in the company of my mother, Audrey, and wife, Gloria, was in honour of my father's name, military regiment, and photograph being placed on the wall in the Dieppe Museum, alongside the other heroes of the Royal Canadian Regiment who fought at Puys. It was a profound closure to a long-standing misnomer. My only regret was that my father had not been alive to enjoy the recognition.

As he got over the passing of my father and his Scoutmaster, Buckshot continued operating his firewood business, which seemed to take a considerable amount of his time. He and his wife were also quite involved in buying and selling with their garage sale activities, and all four of us would take off at daybreak on a bright Saturday morning looking for treasures. The three of them knew that I was not really enamored with other people's stuff, having spent my life in uniform and living a more confined life at sea. However, I went along because the four of us enjoyed being together.

It was absolutely impossible for Buckshot to pass up a bargain. He would phone me at the most inopportune times and ask me to run off somewhere so that I could help him carry, push, or drag someone else's pre-owned stuff home.

His half-acre yard was full of rusting bikes, falling-apart cars, and hundreds of motors, gears, parts, bottles, jugs, and anything else that he thought might eventually make him an extra buck.

He was obsessive with buying and selling stuff, and his garage and car park were full of hundreds of boxes filled with everything ever made. His side yard was littered with boats, motorcycles, and broken and rusting machinery and it became necessary to grow a twelve-foot hedge of trees in the front yard so that the neighbour's would stop spying. A garage sale purchase that greatly pleased Buckshot was a huge white metal torpedo bomb, complete with a top fin that sat on the ground in the entrance to his yard.

In addition, he was bringing logging truck-loads of logs to his backyard so that he could buck and split them into firewood, which he sold and delivered for an astronomical price. He was indeed an entrepreneur.

The good thing about his obsession was that if you needed something, there was a good chance that he had it in his backyard; the problem was finding it when you needed it. He used to get so frustrated when someone asked him if he had a starter for a particular boat motor; he would excitedly say, "Yes, it's in the backyard." Hours later, still hunting for the starter, Buckshot, in absolute frustration, would say, "I know it's here. I just saw it the other day." Unfortunately, he would not quit looking, even after the person had left the property and gone home.

In all truthfulness, Buckshot's house was filled with valuable antiques. He had a door in his dining room that was handmade with multi-colored stained glass windows at the top. When the sun shone through the windows, it was breathtaking. In fact, his whole house was full of beautiful antique furniture. Weighing the facts, the things in the backyard was a drop in the bucket considering the value of his other possessions. From the tender age of eleven, I had been watching Buckshot collect and amass valuable items.

One day, the four of us—Buckshot, Cheryll, Gloria, and I—went to a garage sale at a multi-dwelling complex in Victoria. The whole neighbourhood had dumped fifty years' worth of unwanted possessions on a long row of wobbly tables, and everyone, with the exception of me, was rummaging through the items. Rightfully so, I was bored, tired, and did not want to get my hands dirty from the well-used stuff. Anyhow, I dearly loved my friends, and I managed to refrain from being a party pooper.

About an hour later, wishing that we could go, I saw Buckshot beckoning me over to a table littered with restaurant items: old glass sugar containers, well used napkin holders, and a dozen or so glass salt and pepper shakers.

The seller proudly advised us that he had bought a "box lot" of goodies from a café that went out of business. He was asking twenty-five cents for the shakers. I looked over at Buckshot and noticed that he had something wrapped in his huge right hand. His hands were quite obvious, as not only were they big, but they were also permanently stained with grease and callouses from a lifetime of hard work. Glancing again at his hand he casually opened his fist, and sitting in the middle of his paw was a pair of glass salt and pepper shakers. Opening his hand flat, he pushed his arm forward and said to the guy behind the table, "How much for the salt and pepper shakers?"

With a knowing nod, the seller replied, "Fifty cents each."

Fascinated by the ritual of bartering for junk, I snickered, and Buckshot, maintaining direct eye contact with the haggler, said, "How about twenty-five cents for the pair?" With a smile, the seller agreed, and took the quarter from Buckshot's left hand.

By that time I was really getting bored, so I maneuvered Buckshot towards his parked van.

"Johnnycakes, do you have any idea how much these items are worth?" expostulated my friend of too-many garage sales.

"No, Buckshot. Tell me how much they are worth," I said in exasperation.

"Well, they are really valuable, because they are from the Ming dynasty."

In absolute awe, I patted him on the shoulder in appreciation of his being able to recognize them amongst all the other items. It took me a while to understand the art of garage sale bartering, as I would have probably told the seller they were worth hundreds of dollars and lost out on a "good deal." Now I was really convinced that I did not possess the qualities required of a true collector.

Chapter 9
Turn Island

As the years marched on, Buckshot and I began turning into "grumpy old men," according to our wives; what a compliment that was, considering that Hollywood made millions of dollars on the movie starring Jack Lemmon and Walter Matthau.

Now that we seemed to have more time on our hands to enjoy the fruits of our labor, Buckshot wanted to spend as much time as possible on his island. Unfortunately, getting to Turn Island was a full day traveling in addition to packing and toting our gear. Thinking back, we had been packing and toting gear and groceries into fishing and hunting camps all our lives.

Late one nasty November evening in 2006, I received a telephone call from Buckshot wanting to know if I had the time to go with him to his island for a few days. Being self-employed with a reliable manager and a wife as a business partner meant that I could leave on short notice. My Security Manager, Karl, had served thirty-four years in the Navy and was totally reliable. We were blessed to have him in our company. In addition, Gloria was our surveillance investigator, and she always had files on the go, thereby giving me the time to travel with Buckshot, which she encouraged knowing that being with him was always good for my spirit.

In the wee hours of the morning, we headed north. Because of the remoteness of his island, we always carried our hunting rifles in the winter months, as wolves regularly swam across to the island from East Thurlow, and Buckshot did not want them harassing the deer that frequently inhabited the upper part of the island.

Being November, it was nearly dark when we arrived at Rock Bay, the small inlet twenty-six kilometers east from the turnoff on the highway northeast of Campbell River.

The challenge now was finding a boat to take us to the island, as Buckshot had taken his runabout aluminum boat home last time we were in the area. Upon arriving at the landing, we noticed that the trailer park boys were sitting around in lawn chairs before a blazing campfire.

The flames were quite high, and the guys, who we had known for years, seemed to be into the ale. Buckshot had been logging in the area for years and had a good relationship with some of men sitting there—but not all of them. The biggest and most abrasive was Moose, a former logger who thought that he knew everything about logging, islands, and thieves.

The fellow sitting beside Moose was a fairly quiet little chap from England named John. I always liked John, as we enjoyed talking about our extended families still living in Britain. He was good-natured, and I wanted to talk with him about what had been happening on the island. Of course, Moose wanted to take charge and invited Buckshot to join them for a drink. I had no problem dealing with Moose; however, Buckshot was very private and did not want to talk about his island. Keeping back and away from the firelight, I deferred to my friend.

Although I was known as the professional investigator, Buckshot made short work of Moose and quickly learned that some boaters had tied up at the rear of the island and started a fire, followed by a dozen or so rifle shots. The news greatly disturbed my friend, and edging around and into the firelight, I knelt down beside John and asked him if we could borrow his boat. He immediately agreed, and I went down to the beach and readied the boat for the trip across the straits.

After loading all our gear, I called Buckshot. Several minutes later, we headed out onto the water in the brisk November waves. Passing my flashlight to Buckshot we headed across the channel. It took us about fifteen minutes to get past the front of the island and turn into the boat dock. It was very windy, and we had difficulty in tacking right to clear the front of his island.

Using the flashlight to guide us around the curve and into the log wharf, we both noticed at the same time that the makeshift dock was gone, and that the boom and heavy chains were nowhere to be found.

Struggling to get the boat up on the beach in the dark and at high tide was exhausting, and the grim look on my companion's face told me to keep any comments to myself.

Finally, after about ten minutes of fighting the surging tide, we landed on the rugged beach. Moving all the gear up onto the beach was a chore, as we had to unload everything on the kelp beds and then carry it up the embankment to the trailer. All the while, Buckshot said nothing. Reaching the trailer, I shone my light up the stairs and saw that the place had been trashed. Kicking the debris out of the way, we made our way into the trailer.

Pots, pans, mattresses, glass, and everything else that had been in the trailer was either broken or strewn on the floor. Some of the rear bedroom windowpanes were smashed out, and the woodstove had been pulled off its concrete base. It was beyond our comprehension how anyhow could cause so much need-less destruction.

My lifelong friend was devastated and kept muttering that he should have hired a watch-man to live on the island. Together, we lifted the woodstove back onto the concrete pad so that we could at least keep warm for the night. Covering the broken windows with some old blankets improved the comfort level in the trailer. Within the hour, we had a roaring fire and the warmth slowly permeated throughout the small trailer. Bringing our bedrolls and the rest of the gear in from the porch, we settled down for the night.

The daylight was not as forgiving as the dark, and the damage was even worse than we had thought the night before; however, by the end of the day, the place looked a bit more habitable. Now I understood why Buckshot's wife had refused to move back to the remote and rugged island, as being stuck out in the straits with only a boat and limited amenities was definitely for the young of heart. She had indeed done her time on the island.

Later that afternoon, we made a decision to walk the island and see how much damage had really been done. The first stop was the gen-erator shed. No surprise there, as the generator had been ripped from the pallet and was lying a few feet away. The next stop was the woodshed, which had also been robbed of everything with the exception of a few pieces of firewood. Hoping that the drinking well would be okay, we pulled up a bucket of water. Thankfully, we had fresh water.

Going back to the trailer, I loaded my .308 Winchester rifle, filled my jacket pocket with shells, and started up the gravel road to the top of the Island. Buckshot had run his excavator up the hill about twelve years earlier, and the grade was about eight degrees. Chuffing to the top, which was about an eighth of a mile, we came out onto the granite landing. At the very top there was a tree that looked like a cactus: standing straight up with two bare branches out either side. Looking out across the plateau, the view was spectacular. We could see the curve of the straits as far as the lighthouse south of Rock Bay. Sitting on a stump, we took in the panoramic view. Buckshot had logged the island about fifteen years earlier, and the shrub pines were beginning to grow back.

While sitting there taking in the view and incredible beauty, Buckshot shared that the granite plateau that we were sitting on was worth millions of dollars. He explained that if we could cut the granite out in sheets and lower the sheets down the cliff onto a barge, we could sell a barge load for hundreds of thousands of dollars. The type of granite was very rare, and a company in the United States wanted as much of the granite as he could supply. The difficult part was that the cost of extracting the granite was financially prohibitive. He would need a significant amount of money to extract millions of dollars' worth of granite. The figures were mind-boggling, but there was nothing he could do, as we did not have any hope of getting the development money together. "So close, but so far," was the way he described the situation.

***

On the way back down the hill to the trailer, Buckshot and I walked to the very front of the island where there was about ten acres of perfectly flat and useable land. It was a beautiful spot, and it sat nestled in small alder trees. The beach in front of the site was sandy and a good place to subdivide into five or six-10-acre parcels. Buckshot turned to me and said, "I want to give you and Gloria the choice of one of these proposed lots so that we can build a fishing resort here and grow old hunting and fishing." It was a generous offer, but I knew that our wives would not take to the remoteness of the island; the island was a woodsman's lifestyle.

Later that afternoon, just before dark, we decided to take our rifles and run over to East

Thurlow Island, as we had heard the wolves howling the night before and wanted to scare them out of the area. Setting off just before dark, we tied the boat up across the bay and started walking up a gravel logging road. The road was a steady incline, and after about an hour we got hungry. My companion was always looking to me for our rudimentary needs and asked, "Did you bring something to chew on?"

With a chuckle, I pulled two large Coffee Crisp chocolate bars from my coat pocket. He took one look at the extra-large bars, and turning away from me, proceeded to read me the riot act: "You have known me for most of your life. Don't you know that I hate coffee, and that the smell of coffee makes me sick?"

Well, you could have blown me over with a feather. Not to be discouraged, I defended the chocolate bars: "You love chocolate, that's why I bought them. Here, have one—it will give you some energy."

Again, I was shocked by his response. "I hate coffee, Johnnycakes, why would I eat a Coffee Crisp?" Not being daunted, I ate them both. I love Coffee Crisp chocolate bars.

After a while, Buckshot forgot about my inconsideration (or lack of foresight) with the snack, and we started walking back down the logging road. Halfway down, it started to snow and very quickly became pitch-dark.

As we were slogging down the road towards the boat and I was still trying to justify the chocolate bar fiasco, Buckshot grabbed my arm and told me to be quiet. Thinking that I had gone too far with the chocolate bar story, I started speaking in my defense.

"Listen," Buckshot said. "I hear something following us. It might be wolves. They're curious and will follow behind, stop when we stop, then move again as we move. Load your gun and make lots of noise."

Jacking a shell into my rifle, I started talking loudly and scraping my feet on the gravel as we quickly moved towards the beach. We finally located the boat and took off for his island.

***

The next morning, after a coffee for me and a tea for Buckshot, we headed back to East Thurlow Island. Sure enough, the logging road was covered with wolf tracks, and we could see where the wolves had stopped when we stopped.

Shivering, I went back to the boat. As we were crossing the bay, he told me that when he had been logging further up the coast in a remote area, he had seen wolves and cougars watching him from the timberline, and that he always kept his rifle loaded and in the cab of the machine.

At around 3:30 that afternoon, it stopped snowing and turned to rain. Buckshot was snoozing near the potbellied woodstove, and I decided to take a hike up to the granite plateau and see if I could get a deer. As I was leaving the trailer, Buckshot opened his eyes and said, "Get two, so we can each take one home. There are two big bucks that hang out on the ledge before you get to the top. Now go gettim." Before I left the trailer, he was back asleep.

Creeping up the long incline to the top, I kept my rifle under my rain slicker so that the scope would not be all wet if I had to shoot. Laughing at my fastidiousness, I realized that my eyeglasses were soaking wet and thought about inventing small wiper blades that could clean my glasses when hunting in the rain.

As I turned the corner near the top of the road, I spotted two huge deer standing side by side on the ledge. They were a large buck and smaller doe, and the buck looked to weigh about 180 pounds. Slowly wiping off my wet glasses, I eased my .308 Winchester out from under my slicker. It was raining so hard that the water was cascading down my face and off the yellow slicker.

Bracing my feet and aiming a little above the front shoulder of the buck on the left, I fired. With utter confusion, I looked where they were standing and neither one had moved. It began to rain harder, somehow, and I took aim again and fired two more shots. Still, nothing moved, and they both stood in the same spot. Reloading another three shells, I took aim, fired another shot, and they still stood in the same place. On the last shot, I saw a piece of wood fly up beside the buck's front hoof. Finally noticing me, they leapt up, jumped over the stump, and disappeared behind the ridge.

Reeling back to the trailer in a blowing rainstorm and soaking wet from having opened my slicker several times to reload my rifle, I tramped up the stairs, walked in the door, and noticed that Buckshot was still snoozing by the fire. Without opening his eyes, he drawled, "You must have wiped out the whole herd with that many shots." I did not respond, and Buckshot went back to sleep. Surprisingly, he did not mention the hunt when he woke up later.

***

The following year, while back on the island, Buckshot said that he wanted to go over to the lighthouse south of Rock Bay. Jumping in the boat on a warm sunny September afternoon, we headed off for the point.

On the way, Buckshot advised me that the lighthouse keeper's wife liked to sunbathe, and that out of courtesy we should call from the wharf before stepping foot on the rocks. Tying up at the government wharf, I was once again overwhelmed with the pristine beauty of the lighthouse property. To my delight, Steve had a beautiful forty-three foot sailboat tied up at the wharf, and he had been re-rigging the boat for a summer sea voyage.

The buildings were painted brilliant white, and the rocks were covered with bright green moss. The actual lighthouse was a round white tower standing about a hundred feet in the air. The top portion was painted red, and the flashing beacon stared out to sea. As a sailor, I could envision ships floundering in a raging storm and the lifesaving beacon beckoning them to safety. I loved the beauty and seclusion of the station and kept asking Steve, the Station Master, "When are you going to retire?" I would have taken over immediately, as my secret desire after leaving the Navy was to live and work in a lighthouse.

After about thirty minutes of wandering around the grounds, it was apparent that Steve and his wife were never going to leave their post. The station was manicured to perfection, with a large vegetable garden growing in the sun. The place was shipshape, and just as I was going to sit on the rocks, look out to sea, and daydream about my lighthouse, Buckshot hollered my name.

Returning to the lighthouse, Steve told us that he wanted to go hunting for a few hours, and asked if we would like to go with him. Without preamble, Steve and Buckshot jumped in the truck, and I got into the rear box of the vehicle.

Driving around the recent logging camp slash, the men chatted in the cab while I road hunted. Just before dark, Steve stopped the truck and cracked a beer for them. Sitting in the box of the pickup drinking a coffee, I spotted a small group of deer about fifty yards into the bush. Tapping on the rear window of the cab, I pointed to the deer grazing off to my right. They kept on talking as I started shooting.

After three shots, Buckshot stuck his head out the window of the passenger side and expostulated, "Must be a pile of deer out there now?"

Before I could get down from the back of the truck, Steve jumped out and started slogging away in the bush. It was nearly dark, and I waited patiently for him to give me a status report on the shooting spree.

About five minutes later, in total darkness, I yelled to Steve, "Did you find the deer?"

Whereas he responded in a clear voice that carried back to the truck, "Yeah, I'm standing right beside them and can grab the tail of a doe three feet from me."

Thinking that he was joking, I yelled back, "What are you talking about? I know I hit the buck standing beside the big rock." Knowing that deer will not move in the dark, it made sense that Steve was standing beside them near the rock. Steve offered no response, and suddenly appeared back at the truck and drove off. They totally ignored me for the next half an hour, and Buckshot made no further comments about the incident. Twice now since the previous winter, I had shot my .308 and missed. This was odd, as I had qualified as a marksman in the military.

After pondering the situation, I finally realized that I had changed the scope on the rifle the year before, and obviously the scope was defective. I shared this theory to Buckshot when we got back to the island, and he only grunted. The matter was dropped until I gave the rifle to my grandson David, who confirmed that the scope was in fact defective.

Chapter 10
The New Fishing Boat

Over the next several years, Buckshot and I continued our semi-annual trips to his island on fishing trips and hunting expeditions. When we were unable to go to Turn Island, we went fishing at Port Renfrew, off the outside coast of Vancouver Island. Renfrew is a First Nations and former logging village about two hours west of Victoria, where the San Juan River meets the ocean and faces directly south to the American coast. The channel is in the Straits of Juan de Fuca, and the area where we wanted to fish is referred to as Swiftsure Banks. Unfortunately, Canadians are not permitted to fish in that area.

Some of the best fishing on Vancouver Island is in the Pacific Ocean along the southwest coast. It is also very windy and generally wet, and the ground swells are extremely danger-ous. Fog is also a common dilemma in August and September and makes fishing in the straits very hazardous. The faint of heart are encouraged to hire fishing guides.

Since 1958, Buckshot had always owned second-hand fishing boats with the exception of "nearly new" Double Eagle boats that seemed to have disappeared for no explainable reason. My fishing boats are a different story and Buckshot would rather take his boat fishing as it was rigged for the deep sea and came with electric downriggers, heavy cannon balls, scads of crab traps, and red and white float buoys.

Buckshot loved dropping crab traps in the water no matter where we fished. If we went to Crofton, just east of Duncan, he would drop the traps down and hook a rope to a red and white floater buoy with his name and fishing number. Coming back from a day of fishing, I would laboriously hand haul the traps to the surface while he sorted the crabs out and threw the undersized ones back in the sea. Reaching home, we would have a fish and crab BBQ. His chest freezers were always full of halibut and salmon.

Around the summer of 2004, Buckshot started hinting about maybe selling his island. I did not take him seriously, as he constantly talked about how much he loved Turn Island. The purchase of the island had been a lifelong dream. However, we were getting older, and the trips to the island were becoming further and further apart. It was also becoming a burden protecting the island from thieves and vandals.

We continued fishing at Port Renfrew and taking trips to the United States with our wives, and one day, out of the blue, he came to my office where I was working and told me that he had an offer for his island.

"When did you list the island?" I asked.

"It's not listed, but this realtor in the area called me and said he knew a client who was interested," Buckshot told me.

The news took me by surprise, and we went for a drive to discuss the offer. I knew how much he loved Turn Island and could not fathom why he would consider a sale. During our drive, he hinted that his family was concerned about how dangerous it was to be on the secluded island in the wintertime and was suggesting that maybe he should sell. It was a difficult decision to make, and I offered no opinion.

Several months later, I learned that he had sold the island to an American from Hawaii who, as a condition of sale, had promised not to develop the island into a commercial enterprise. The buyer agreed, and Buckshot sold the island. He was never the same after selling his island which was a topic of regret for the next several years.

***

For more than twenty-two years, between 1990 and 2012, Buckshot, our wives and I played hours of canasta or euchre at either their home or ours. It was wonderful, and we spent most of the time laughing about everything and anything that came to mind. We clicked as a foursome, and it was great to have such wonderful friends.

Buckshot had amassed a huge collection of rocks, trinkets, marbles, and relics over the years, and every card game was preceded by a showing of his most recent acquisitions. It was delightful watching Buckshot lay out his treasures on the kitchen table. Each and every item was lovingly caressed by him as he explained how and where he had found the trinket. One day, while we were sitting at his kitchen table, he reached behind himself and dug something out of the antique roll top desk where he kept some of his recent finds.

Turning back in his chair, he placed an old and well-used painted metal rum mug on the table. The mug depicted a salty bearded sailor drinking Navy grog. I was overwhelmed, as I had not seen one of those mugs since the Navy unified in 1968. Buckshot regularly bought my wife and me things at garage sales that he knew we liked. It was very endearing, and at the same time very tender, considering that he was a tough old woodsman.

In 2008, I was elected President of Cowichan Branch 53, Royal Canadian Legion in Duncan. I had been a member of the Legion since 1966 and devoted considerable time on Executive Committees in Legions all across Canada.

In October 2009, in the second year of my presidency, I had the occasion to attend at Government House in Victoria for a First Poppy Presentation by a First Nations Lieutenant Governor, the Honorable Steven Point.

While standing in the Receiving Line waiting for the Lieutenant Governor to address the small Legion group, the Lieutenant Governor looked at my service medals and asked me about my military career.

Without hesitation, I told him that while stationed at the Canadian Forces School of Intelligence and Security in Borden, Ontario, in 1980, the now-retired Captain George Bull (a friend of mine) and myself were tasked to start the first All Native Cadet Corps (as it was referred to at that time) in Canada. The Corps was started on Christian Island, a small Island in the Georgian Bay, near Penetanguishene, Ontario. Christian Island was the only Indian Reserve in Canada that was comprised of Seven Nations of Indigenous people. I took this opportunity to share my vision of starting a First Nations Cadet Corps in the Cowichan Valley; this was to be the first such Corps in British Columbia.

With a radiant smile, the Lieutenant Governor grasped my hand in both of his, leaned in towards me, and confided that he been a Cadet, and that if this could be done he would attend the inaugural service of the Corps.

In consultation with Navy Commander Rod Hughes, Commanding Officer Regional Cadet Support (Pacific), and Chief Lydia Hwitsum, Chief of Cowichan Tribes, we successfully launched the 2925 (Khowutzun) Royal Canadian Army Cadet Corps the following summer. True to his word, the Lieutenant Governor officially opened the Corps in the Siem Lelum Gym and Hall during its first Annual Parade.

With tears trickling down his face, the Honorable Steven Point shared, "I was also a Cadet, and now I am the Lieutenant-Governor of BC, and you First Nations cadets can also be anything you want to be as well." He then presented the Corps with the Lieutenant Governor's pin to be worn proudly on their uniform lapels and officially adopted the Corps as the "Lieutenant Governor's Own Cadet Corps", proudly displaying their Corps photo on his government web page. To my delight, Buckshot and I attended the opening ceremony, and for the second time in our lives, we attended an official gathering with the Cowichan Tribes.

To my utter surprise and delight, I received an official letter from Government House in March 2012, inviting me to a presentation ceremony to receive the Diamond Jubilee Medal for my part in launching the Cadet Corps.

***

After selling Turn Island, Buckshot bought a twenty-eight-foot trophy fishing boat with forward sleeping quarters, a head, and two 175-horse-power motors complete with a 9.9 kicker. It was a beautiful boat, and his plan was to set up a travel trailer in the First Nations campground at Port Renfrew.

We took the trailer to Renfrew, and for a fee of six hundred dollars parked the trailer until the end of October. It was ideal, and he could moor his boat in the San Juan River, directly in front of the campsite. For the next two years, we spent many, many days and nights fishing and camping at Port Renfrew.

On one such fishing trip, we took my twelve-year-old grandson David to the trailer. In fact, we had been taking David with us on many day trips since he was eight years old, and he was turning into a seasoned salt-water fisher-man. Off we went and moved into the trailer for a three-day fishing adventure. David was very fond of Buckshot, and the three of us became fishing partners.

On the second day out and in late August, the fog rolled in as we were heading out into the straits. The tide was low, and we had to navigate the large and deep hulled boat down the river and into the channel. David was up front, I was on the port side, and Buckshot was driving the boat. We had about six inches of water to spare under the keel as we neared the entrance to the straits. With both motors high out of the water with just enough water circulating through the cooling system to keep the motors from heating up, we surged into the channel and Buckshot opened her up as we sped towards the crab trap buoys. After lowering the crab traps in about two hundred feet of water, we headed out to the fishing grounds where Buckshot said he wanted me to take over control of the kicker motor using the remote steering line; a hand held cable about six feet long that was electronically wired to the small motor.

We were fishing close to the craggy shore for spring salmon and I was having difficulty maneuvering in the fog and staying out of the kelp beds. The tide was ebbing and the spring salmon, which usually weighed between twenty-five and forty pounds, were thought to be feeding in the floating kelp beds.

The New Fishing Boat

At around 10:30 a.m., while twisting and turning in an attempt to keep out of the kelp and at the same time stay alongside the kelp beds, Buckshot hooked a spring salmon. At the same time, David, who was told to my take rod out of the stern holder, also hooked a spring salmon, and everything suddenly changed.

"David," yelled Buckshot, "Hang on tight, and don't let go of the rod and Johnnycakes, keep the boat straight and don't let the prop get caught in the kelp." It was foggy, damp, and chaotic. Suddenly, I looked up and saw David being pulled back towards the stern.

My grandson began yelling at me to do something as he skidded towards the stern of the heaving boat. I dropped the steering cable and rushed over to grab him while he was flat on his behind and being dragged towards the back. I knew that David was not going to let go of the rod and feared that he would be pulled over the stern and into the churning sea.

Buckshot turned, saw David starting to go over the back of the boat, and reaching over with his big meaty hand grabbed David's belt at the top of his pants. Buckshot was now holding a fishing rod in his right hand and David with a fish on the line in his left hand; meanwhile, I was trying to save my grandson from going overboard while keeping the boat out of the kelp beds and off the rocks at the same time.

The boat was beginning to turn circles in the fog, so Buckshot shoved David down on the deck and told him to brace both feet against the inside of the transom. Minutes later, Buckshot had his fish in the boat and grabbed the rod from David who was smiling but exhausted.

Buckshot reeled the salmon to the starboard side of the boat and showed David how to safely net the fish. When the second fish was in the boat and flopping around on the deck, David grabbed a large lead-weighted fish bonker and proceeded to whack his fish.

Seeing David smashing at the fish, Buckshot yelled, "David, don't hit the floor of the boat. Hit the fish." There were fiberglass chips flying everywhere, and just as I was going to grab David's arm, Buckshot reached for the fish bonker and received a hard whack on the wrist.

About ten minutes later, we got organized and headed back to shore. On the way we stopped at the crab traps, hauled the traps up into the boat, while keeping only the legal-sized crabs.

***

That night, when everyone had calmed down, we laughed while telling the story about bringing the two fish into the boat while twisting around in the kelp beds. We thoroughly enjoyed eating fresh crabmeat and hot dogs around the campfire. David's eyes were the size of saucers, and to this day, he still brags about catching and netting his very first twenty-eight-pound spring salmon and whacking Buckshot on the wrist. After fishing and camping at Port Renfrew for the next few years, the campground closed and we had to take the boat on day runs only.

On a particularly hot and dry July day in 2009, we took his boat to Port Renfrew. The gravel road was very dry, and the loose gravel offered little purchase on the steep switchback roads. At around noon, and while driving back to Mesachie Lake, we were struggling to get up a rather steep switchback when the passenger side trailer wheel bearing burned out and the boat nearly came off the trailer. Stuck out on the logging road about thirty kilometers from civilization, we needed to make a decision what we were going to do with the $80,000 boat. Seeing that Buckshot did not want to leave the boat on the side of the road, I volunteered to stay with the boat so that he could go back home and get a six-ton hydraulic jack and a wheel bearing set.

About four hours later, Buckshot came back and we spent the next two hours in the dark fixing the wheel bearing so we could get his boat back home. It became apparent that the trailer was not big enough for the boat.

About six weeks later, we learned that the annual sockeye run was going to be announced shortly by the Fisheries Department, so we made plans to fish in the inside passage. Several days later, I got a midnight call from Buckshot who told me that the sockeye run was on for one day only, and that we had to leave for Port Alberni at 3:00 a.m. the next morning.

David happened to be staying over for the night, so we raced off to Port Alberni to catch the early morning run in the Port Alberni Inlet. The only problem was that we had to take my fifteen-foot aluminum boat with the 9.9-horsepower motor, as Buckshot's boat was in the water at Cowichan Bay while the trailer was being rebuilt.

Port Alberni is approximately three hours northwest from Duncan, and when we arrived at the boat launch, the place was crowded. Boats of all sizes were lined up at the launch and daylight was burning.

In addition, the First Nations Fisheries Control from the Nuu-chah-nulth Tribal Council was recording everyone's name and directing that all catches had to be registered upon returning to the boat ramp. The official name of the First Nations organization is the Port Alberni Uu-a-thluk aquatic resource management, which means "taking care of" as it relates to natural resources and aquatic habitat.

Hours later, we got out on the water, and in the blistering heat chugged up and down the channel trying to catch sockeye. In the rush to leave, I had forgotten to bring my two fishing rod downriggers, so Buckshot fell asleep on the middle seat, David operated the motor, and I crawled up front and covered my head with a windbreaker. It was the first time since knowing Buckshot that we had been skunked.

Finally, at around 3:30 p.m., exhausted and burning from the hot sun, we headed in and spent two hours trying to get onto the boat ramp. To our dismay and Buckshot's obvious annoyance, every boat that came in was loaded with sockeye.

Pulling out of the boat launch, we parked across the street and took David for fish and chips. It was the only thing we could do considering our dismal fishing trip. The next day, the season closed. We had missed the one opportunity to load up with sockeye.

Chapter 11
Growing Older

The following year, in 2010 we spent most of the summer at Port Renfrew. I noticed that Buckshot was experiencing severe cramping in his hands and forearms. "Buckshot, what is happening to your hands?" I asked out of concern.

The ever-private Buckshot mumbled, "It's from all the years of operating a power saw, and each cramp seems to take more and more massaging to work out the spasms."

I was concerned with his answer, as he was a proud and self-reliant man, and my insistence that something was wrong only made him more sullen.

The cramping in his arms became more frequent, and my concerns increased. After one rather long episode of spasms, he asked me to take over control of the boat—something that he rarely did, as he loved running his boat. At the time we were across from the Swiftsure

Bank in the Straits of Juan de Fuca and fishing for halibut on the Canadian side of the international border. I backed the boat in near the huge bell buoy so that we could drift with the tide and lowered our fishing lines to the bottom. After an hour of peace and quiet, and drifting in the afternoon breeze, I got some goodies out of the cooler and we started eating lunch. Minutes later, Buckshot hooked a huge halibut.

Halibut can weigh anywhere from 30 to 170 pounds and take considerable effort to bring into the boat. Afraid of tangling our lines, I reeled my line in and asked Buckshot if I could help him with his fish, as I could see that he was struggling. His huge hands were cramped, and the pain on his face was breaking my heart.

"No," said my friend of many, many years. "I'll be all right." Fifteen minutes later, he was still struggling with the fish and commented, "This halibut is like pulling up a sheet of plywood, you'll have to cut my line."

For the second time since meeting Buckshot, I was confused by his request. I'd seen him play a forty-five pound "Tyee" (Nuu-chah-nulth, meaning king, chief or champion) spring salmon in the Campbell River Straits for hours without uttering a single complaint. Grabbing a fish knife out of the tackle box, I cut the line. He immediately sat down and started rubbing his arms.

Concerned for my friend, I drove the boat back to the launch and left him with the boat at the dock while I went and got his truck. This was the first time in our years of fishing that he could not bring the boat in by himself. I didn't particularly like his one-ton truck, as the clutch was worn and difficult to shift, especially when backing down a steep boat ramp at low tide.

As I turned into the boat ramp, I noticed him trying to hold the boat against the wharf. The water was shallow, and I was concerned that I wouldn't be able to get the boat onto the trailer without help. Buckshot was unusually subdued and not offering any suggestions.

Backing down the ramp and into the water, I took the truck out of gear, set the brake, and jumped to the ground. The wind started to come up, and I could see him standing on the bow of his twenty-eight-foot boat with a pained look on his face. If I did not get the boat up soon, the wind might push it against the wharf, and I would have a difficult time getting it out of the water.

Rolling up my trouser legs, I waded into the water, grabbed the bowline, and started winching the boat onto the trailer. With a lot of effort, I hauled the boat up, jumped back in the truck, and drove into the parking lot. As I got out of the truck, I immediately smelled the clutch burning. Buckshot was still sitting on the front of his boat and casually commented, "You left the emergency brake on, and I can smell the clutch. Tie the boat down so we can get out of here."

After leaving the boatyard, I drove the truck to his house. Buckshot was still rubbing his arm and not saying much, and when he went into the house still rubbing his arm, his daughter Brenda did some research on the internet and suggested that prolonged arm cramping could be the result of dehydration.

The cramping continued on and off over the next few months, and I noticed that he was having difficulty cutting and stacking firewood. Not wanting to alarm me, Buckshot said nothing more about the problem.

One Saturday morning, he called me and asked if I would help him with his firewood. I gladly agreed, and went to his house. He was thin, weak, and refused to talk about his health. It was at that time that I learned he was taking chemotherapy and getting dialysis in Victoria. Everyone but me knew that Buckshot was ill, and it had a profound effect on me.

Several weeks later, he called me and said that he had bought a small boat at a garage sale; he asked me if I would like to go with him to the lake and try it out. I was delighted to go, and I went to his house and loaded the boat into the back of the truck. As we left, I noticed that his Trophy fishing boat was still sitting where he had left it months before.

His dog Shelia, a blue heeler cross who rarely left his side, was sitting on the front seat of his truck while I loaded the boat. After securing the boat, we departed and headed out on some back roads. Not knowing why he was driving away from the lake, I had the temerity to ask where we were going. His response confused me even more: "We're going to a small lake on Glenora Road."

I was more confused than ever, and I continued asking him questions about the mysterious lake, which I had no idea existed. Finally, after an interminable amount of time, we drove down a bumpy road, came to a ditch, and then a small and reedy pond. The supposed lake looked like a farmer's watering pond.

He asked me to back the truck down to the water, and I then lowered the boat to the ground. He extracted two small brass plugs from his jacket pocket and inserted them in the rear of the eight-foot homemade boat. We shoved the boat into the pond, and to my surprise, the dog jumped in the boat and Buckshot told me to climb in as well. I crawled in the rocking and insecure watercraft as he pushed off from the grass and jumped in beside the dog.

We went about six feet into the pond, and both plugs popped out of the holes and the boat began to sink.

It was early October and quite cool. Anyhow, the boat sank, the dog abandoned ship, and Buckshot and I sat up to our waist in the water. We had now gone full circle in our fishing careers. I learned on the way home that Buckshot had paid twenty-five dollars for the boat at a garage sale and wanted to know if it would float. That was the last time I was in a boat with Buckshot. He was sixty-four that year.

The following May in 2011, on my sixty-fourth birthday, I was hired as a Command Service Officer working through the Legion Service Bureau with Veterans Affairs Canada. I had been a volunteer Veterans Advocate for over thirty years, and this new full-time job put me back on the Military Base at CFB Esquimalt— the same base where I had started my sailing career in 1966.

Buckshot was not pleased that I had gone to work in Victoria and kept complaining that it was time for retirement. Although we still owned our investigations company, we only took the cases that we wanted. My preference at that time was criminal defence work, and my wife enjoyed doing surveillance files. Both types of cases were lucrative, and earning a good income was not an issue.

Buckshot and I still continued to spend as much time as we could together when I was not working or traveling with my job. As a Veterans Advocate and Pension Disability Officer, my work took me all over Vancouver Island and occasional trips across the country.

***

In the second year of my employment working with Veterans Affairs, I wrote a comprehensive training package and delivered the program to every province in Canada. I loved the job but I was growing weary and wanted to spend more time with my best friend.

Going part-time in the fall of 2012, five months after my sixty-fifth birthday, I was able to spend more time with Buckshot. He was getting chemotherapy five days a week in Victoria and rapidly losing weight. I was in denial that he was ill and continued to be there if he needed me for anything, as I honestly believed that he was going to recover and be the same energetic buddy I had known for most of my life.

Years earlier, Buckshot and his wife Cheryll had built a huge swimming pool in front of their home. The pool, bathroom cabana, and hot tub enclosure covered the entire width of the front part of their stately home. Our respective grandchildren really enjoyed the pool, tub, and gazebo, and we spent many wonderful after-noons and weekends swimming, tubbing, and

sharing meals, especially after a day of crab-
bing and fishing at Port Renfrew.

Those were wonderful times, and right before
our eyes we watched our grandchildren mature
into young adults. It brought back memories of
our growing up together in the Cowichan Valley.
Our oldest grandson, Keith, did spend some
time with us fishing; however, he was busy in
the black belt program with martial arts and
unfortunately did not get time to experience
many of our fishing adventures.

Chapter 12
The Last Adventure

On February 12, 2013, my wife and I bought a new home in Lake Cowichan—the place where I had gone to elementary school, and where Buckshot had met his future wife, Cheryll. People that I hardly knew in Duncan were telling me that my friend was quite ill, and when I asked Buckshot if everything was all right, he would turn his back and change the subject.

Wanting to show Buckshot our new house in Lake Cowichan, I drove to his place and asked him if he would like to see the house. He looked really tired, and it was suggested by Cheryll that he should stay home. However, Buckshot said he was going with me to the lake, and we headed out in my truck.

Because I was working in Victoria, traveling the island for my job, and not spending enough time with my friend, I had had no idea how ill he had become. Helping him to my truck and getting him into the front seat was painful to see. Arriving at our new home, Buckshot was not strong enough to make it up the inside stairs without resting; however, he managed to see the upstairs from the first landing, as well as the spectacular view of the mountains and the lake. I drove downtown, bought him a small egg and sausage breakfast bun, and then parked at the river where he had met his wife in 1963. He was quiet and subdued and finally told me that he was scheduled for abominable surgery on March 19.

In a cautious voice, I asked Buckshot if he would mind if I talked about eternal life. In a weak and subdued voice he replied, "Yes, I'm okay with that." I shared with him the truth about sin and redemption. After hearing what the Lord had done for us, Buckshot said that he wanted to ask Jesus into his heart.

It was a profound experience, and minutes later, Buckshot invited the Lord Jesus Christ into his heart. I was overjoyed as tears came to my eyes and knew that all was going to be right with Buckshot, and that our adventure together would continue throughout eternity. He seemed at peace and thanked me for standing up for my convictions.

On March 18, he went into the hospital in Victoria and was operated on the next day. My office was only twenty minutes from the hospital, so I spent as many days with him as I could for the next three weeks. Most days when I arrived in the late afternoon he was sleeping, and Cheryll, who had been there since early morning, left and started the long drive back to Duncan. Not wishing to wake him, I curled up on the settee by the window and went to sleep until he stirred. Just being in the same room with him was very comforting, and near the middle of April, Buckshot pleaded with me to get him home so he could be with his family. At the same time, Buckshot said that his surgeon had told him that he might live three more weeks.

That afternoon, I spoke with his surgeon outside in the hallway and told him that my best friend wanted to go home. The young doctor was firm and said that there was not enough time to arrange for home care in Duncan.

I asked, "If I can arrange home care, will you release him to me?"

His response was, "It probably won't happen, but good luck." Within an hour, I had arranged for Buckshot to be transported back to his home the following afternoon.

***

As I was still only working part-time, I was able to spend quality time with him in his home. On one particular day in late April, I asked him if he would like me to read him a story. He was very weak and nodding off and in a deep sleep most of the time. However, on that particular day, he said that he would like me to read to him, and looking around the room, I saw a cowboy book sitting on a shelf across from his cot. Taking the book in my hand, I began reading the story.

Being able to read quickly and change content had always been easy for me from an early age, so I started changing the words so that the cowboy was a sailor and the horse a fishing boat.

It was wonderful to see a smile on his pale and thin face as I read the story about a fishing boat captain hauling in big fish on his boat. I think he knew that I was making up the story, although he said he wanted me to read some more.

After a few minutes of silence, his breathing slowed down and he fell into a deep and peaceful sleep. As I left the room, I leaned over his bed, and for the first time in our many years of friendship, I whispered, "I never said before that I love you, Buckshot."

His quiet response was, "I feel the same way."

***

On May 2, 2013, my best friend of nearly fifty-six years passed away, twenty days before his sixty-seventh birthday. Two days before he passed, I knelt down by his small medical bed, which was sitting on the floor at the end of his large queen-sized bed, and whispered into his ear: "Buckshot—I have only one regret in my life: that I should have listened more and talked less."

He opened his eyes, and the last words I heard from my best friend and lifelong buddy were, "It was just right, Johnnycakes," and after a slight pause, "nothing matters."

Several years later, while looking at his picture leaning against a small container of his ashes on my office desk, I realized it was time to let go of my friend. With resolve in my heart, I walked down to the Cowichan River, and on a grassy bank on the south side of the river spread his ashes into the gently swirling waters.

After hiking for about an hour along the trail on the other side of the river, I returned to where I had sprinkled his ashes, and while walking over the trestle, I looked back and saw the full outline of Buckshot's face on the mossy rocks beneath the gently moving water. With tears in my eyes and a pain in my heart, I looked again, and Buckshot was gone.

Printed in Canada